S0-BTM-026

PRACTICE FOR U.S. CITIZENSHIP AND LEGALIZATION OF STATUS TESTS

PRACTICE FOR U.S. CITIZENSHIP AND LEGALIZATION OF STATUS TESTS

Carlos F. Paz

PRENTICE
HALL
PRESS

New York London Toronto Sydney Tokyo Singapore

Third Edition

Copyright © 1983,1988, 1990 by Arco Publishing, a division
of Simon & Schuster, Inc.
All rights reserved
including the right of reproduction
in whole or in part in any form

 PRENTICE HALL PRESS

Simon & Schuster, Inc.
15 Columbus Circle
New York, NY 10023

An Arco Book
Published by Prentice Hall Press

Prentice Hall Press and colophons are
registered trademarks of Simon & Schuster, Inc.

Manufactured in the United States of America

1 2 3 4 5 6 7 8 9 10

Library of Congress Cataloging-in-Publication Data

Paz, Carlos F.
    Practice for U.S. citizenship and legalization of status tests /
Carlos F. Paz.
        p. cm.
    ISBN 0-13-6911288-5
    1. Citizenship—United States. 2. United States—Politics and
government. 3. Emigration and immigration law—United States.
I. Title. II. Practice for U.S. citizenship and legalization
of status tests.
JK1758.P39 1990
323.6'0973—dc20   90-19504
                                                          CIP

Contents

Preface

What this book is all about:

In brief and simple language this book presents the requirements for naturalization, a short history of the United States and its government, and examples of the kinds of questions you will be asked in the written and oral examinations. The information provided here is not meant to take the place of the United States Immigration and Naturalization Service pamphlets, but simply to give additional help to the men and women who wish to become United States citizens.

This book includes the basic facts, laws, and regulations you need to know to become a citizen, plus over 200 sample questions of the sort used by examiners.

Carlos F. Paz

Overview of the Immigration Reform and Control Act of 1986

The Immigration Reform and Control Act of 1986 was signed into law by President Reagan on November 6, 1986. The key elements of the new law are sanctions against employers who knowingly hire illegal aliens, and legalization of certain qualified illegal aliens.

LEGALIZATION OF UNDOCUMENTED ALIENS

A major part of the new immigration law is legalization of undocumented aliens who meet specific criteria. To be eligible for amnesty, an alien must prove that he/she has had continuous illegal residence in the United States since before January 1, 1982. However, aliens convicted of a felony of three or more misdemeanors lose their chance for legalization. Legalized aliens would be given temporary resident status for eighteen months, after which they have one year to apply for permanent residence. *To become permanent residents, they have to show a minimal understanding of English and U.S. history and government.* After five years as a permanent resident, an alien could apply for citizenship. During that five-year period, an alien would be ineligible for welfare, food stamps, and most other Federal benefits.

The year-long program began on May 5, 1987. As part of the application process, an alien must provide proof of having been in the United States for the five years specified by the law, with the exception of "brief, casual or innocent absences." Such absences can be as much as 45 days for a single period or an aggregate of 180 days during the five-year period.

The permitted length of such absences is less if the illegal alien leaves the country after the regulations were enacted, i.e., May 1, 1986. In such a case, he/she is permitted "brief, casual or innocent absences," which are defined as a single absence of not more than 30 days or an aggregate or not more than 90 days. The current INS policy is that an illegal alien must get INS approval for intended departures from the United States after May 1, 1987 or lose his/her chance for legalization.

To prove that he/she has been here for five years, an applicant for amnesty may show a variety of documents including such items as pay stubs, income tax returns or withholding forms, rent receipts, utility bills or bank statements. The government will favor "employment-related documents," and may require "independent corroboration" of any document. The applicant is also allowed to present "affidavits of credible witnesses" as further evidence on his/her behalf.

To facilitate the registration and legalization process, the INS has designated church and community groups to provide advice to aliens and to assist in the preparation of applications. These groups perform the function of screening alien applications, and will inform those potential applicants who are ineligible for amnesty.

EMPLOYER SANCTIONS

Although it has in the past been illegal for undocumented aliens to work in the United States, it has not, until now, been unlawful for employers to hire these aliens. With the passage of the new immigration law, employers will now be subject to civil penalties and ultimately imprisonment if they "knowingly" hire, recruit or refer for a fee any unauthorized alien. Similarly, it is also unlawful for employers to continue to employ an alien who was hired after November 6, 1986, knowing that he/she was or is unauthorized to work. (An exception is provided for agricultural workers until November 30, 1988.)

According to the schedule of penalties, after an initial citation, an employer will be fined between $250 and $2,000 per alien for a first offense; he will be subject to a fine of $2,000 to $5,000 for his second offense; and will face a fine between $3,000 and $10,000 for the third offense. For "pattern of practice" of particularly flagrant violations, an employer could face criminal penalties up to $3,000 and six months in prison.

To avoid such penalties, the employer must abide by specific verification procedures. The potential employer must require a job applicant to present documents proving his/her identity as well as authorization to work in the U.S. Identity documents could be a driver's license, passport or similar government document with a photograph. "Work authorization" documents could be a social security card, a U.S. birth certificate, or any other document specifically providing proof of work authorization. Documents that fulfill both requirements for a potential employer would be a U.S. passport, a certificate of U.S. citizenship, a certificate of naturalization, an unexpired foreign passport with work authorization, or a "green card" (officially an alien registration card). Until September 1, 1987, employers could hire illegal aliens who planned to apply for amnesty and simply note on the Form I-9 that the illegal alien has said he/she is eligible for amnesty and intends to apply.

DISCRIMINATION

Employers who plan to avoid the potential hassles of hiring aliens by hiring only U.S. citizens will also be in violation of the immigration law's anti-discrimination provisions. It is not unlawful for an employer to choose a U.S. citizen over a non-citizen if the two are equally qualified for the job. However, it is illegal for an employer to discriminate against a legal resident on the basis of citizenship status or national origin.

AGRICULTURAL PROVISIONS

The amnesty conditions in the agricultural industry vary from those in other industries. To be eligible for temporary residency, farmworkers need to have worked in American agriculture for only 90 days between May 1985 and May 1986. There are different timetables for becoming permanent residents, depending on how many seasons farmworkers have worked in the U.S. The new law also provides for replenishment of the seasonal work force by allowing new workers to enter the country as temporary residents if there is a shortage of agricultural workers.

Legalization Fact Sheet

Who Qualifies

Illegal aliens who have lived in the United States since before January 1982 are eligible for legalization, if:

- They have not left the United States since January 1, 1982, except for brief and casual absences. ("Brief" and "Casual" have been determined to mean absences from the United States of not more than 45 days in a single departure and no more than 180 days total in any number of departures.)

- They have never been convicted of a felony or three or more misdemeanors and are otherwise admissible.

Steps Towards Legalization

- Obtain applications, including required medical examination forms, from legalization offices, qualified designated entities, direct service providers, or attorneys. The following fees must accompany the application when it is filed:

  Adults and children $ 80
  Maximum for family $240

  Fees can be paid with a cashier's check, a bank money order or a postal money order. Money orders should be made payable to the U.S. Immigration and Naturalization Service.

- Fill out the application form. Assistance is available from qualified designated entities, direct service providers or attorneys. These people may charge for their services.

- The following must be submitted with the application for each beneficiary.

1. Two passport-type color photographs, 2 inches by 2 inches, available at locations taking passport photographs or qualified designated entities. A specification sheet will be included with the application.

2. Two sets of fingerprints, which can be obtained from volunteer agencies and police departments. Photograph and fingerprint services may be available at some legalization offices.

3. A medical examination form filled out by an approved doctor. A list of approved doctors will be provided with the application.

4. Original documents to prove identity and residency requirements.

   A. Proof of Identity (at least one of following)
      Passport
      Birth Certificate
      National I.D. card
      State drivers license
      Baptismal records/marriage certificate
      Affidavits

   B. Proof of Residence (any two of following)
      Past employment records such as:
         Income tax forms
         Letters from employers
         Letters from banks if self-employed
      Utility bills
      Rental receipts
      School records

- When all documents have been completed, they must be filed at a legalization office. Some locations may require them to be filled in person. No appointment is necessary. Time and hours of individual offices vary.

- When the application is submitted, the applicant will receive an identification document with employment authorization, and a time will be set for an interview.

- If the application is denied, all information will be held in strict confidence except in cases of fraud (documents falsified or forged).

INS Legalization Offices

U.S. IMMIGRATION NATURALIZATION SERVICE DIRECTORY OF LEGALIZATION OFFICES

ALASKA

Michael Building
620 East Tenth Avenue
Suite 10
Anchorage, AK 99510

ARIZONA

3420 South Seventh Street
Phoenix, AZ 85040

1325 West 16th Street
Yuma, AZ 85364

CALIFORNIA

1011 17th Street
Bakersfield, CA 93301

9858 Artesia Boulevard
Bellflower, CA 90706

7342 Orangethorpe Avenue
Buena Park, CA 90621

1627 West Main Street
El Centro, CA 92243

9660 Flair Drive
El Monte, CA 91731

463 North Midway Drive
Escondido, CA 92027

1649 Van Ness Avenue
Fresno, CA 93721

Greenbriar Plaza
12912 Brookhurst Boulevard
Garden Grove, CA 92640

555 Redondo Beach
  Boulevard
Gardena, CA 90248

6022 Santa Fe Avenue
Huntington Park, CA 90255

83-558 Avenue 45, Suite 8
Indio, CA 92201

300 North Los Angeles Street
Los Angeles, CA 90012

1671 Wilshire Blvd,
Los Angeles, CA 90017

1241 South Soto Street
Los Angeles, CA 90022

11307 Vanowen Street
North Hollywood, CA 91605

400 South "A" Street
Oxnard, CA 93030

960 East Holt Avenue
Pomona, CA 91767

1401 Gold Street
Redding, CA 96001

1285 Columbia Avenue
Riverside, CA 92507

3041 65th Street
Sacramento, CA 95820-9000

947 Blanco Circle
Salinas, CA 93901

3247 Mission Village Drive
San Diego, CA 92123

Appraisers Building
630 Sansome Street
San Francisco, CA 94111

1727 Mission Street
San Francisco, CA 94103-
2417

1040 Commercial Street
San Jose, CA 95112

1901 South Ritchey Street
Santa Ana, CA 99501

1575 thru 1577
Suite 15
Stowell Center Plaza
Santa Maria, CA 92705

16921 Parthenia Street
Sepulveda, CA 91343

7475 Murray Drive
Stockton, CA 95210

COLORADO

Albrook Center
4730 Paris Street
Denver, CO 80239

FLORIDA

Jackson Building
601 South Andrews Ave.
Fort Lauderdale, FL 33301

Palm Springs Mile Mall
500 West 49th Street
Hialeah, FL 33012

Post Office Building
311 West Monroe Street, Rm.
227
P.O. Box 4608
Jacksonville, FL 32202

Rotunda Plaza
18922 South Dixie Highway
Miami, FL 33157

North Lake Business Park
2900 Southwest Third
Terrace
Okeechobee, FL 33974

Corporate Square, Suite 625
7402 North 56th Street
Tampa, FL 33617

GEORGIA

1395 Columbia Drive, Suite
A-10
Decatur, GA 30032

GUAM

Pacific News Building
238 O'Hara Street
Agana, GU 96910

IDAHO

Stout Building II
1828 Airport Way
Boise, ID 83705

Exchange Plaza Building
1820 East 17th Street
Idaho Falls, ID 83401

ILLINOIS

Farmsworth Center for
  Business
1050 Corporate Boulevard
Aurora, IL 60504

3119 North Pulaski
Chicago, IL 60641

Crown Oaks Midwest
Ground Floor
1700 West 119th Street
Chicago, IL 60643

Forest Park Mall—Lower
  Level
7600 West Roosevelt Road
Forest Park, IL 60130

IOWA

2720 W. Locust Street
Suite 14
Davenport, IA 52804

MAINE

156 Federal Street
Portland, ME 04101

MARYLAND

U.S. Appraisors Stores
103 South Gay Street
2nd Floor
Baltimore, MD 21202

MASSACHUSETTS

600 Washington Street
Boston, MA 02111

MICHIGAN

333 Mt. Elliot Street
Detroit, MI 48207

MINNESOTA

Alpha Business Center
2700 East 82nd Street
Bloomington, MN 55420

MISSOURI

210 North Tucker Boulevard
Room 100
St. Louis, MO 63101

MONTANA

Professional Plaza Building
900 North Montana
Helena, MT 59601

NEBRASKA

Federal Building
Room 1008
106 South 15th Street
Omaha, NE 68012

NEW JERSEY

30 North Fifth Street
Camden, NJ 08101

Franklin Mill Office Center
22 Mills Street
Paterson, NJ 07501

NEW MEXICO

1900 Bridge Boulevard, S.W.
Albuquerque, NM 87105

NEW YORK

Ansonia Center
712 Main Street at Tupper
Buffalo, NY 14202

VA Federal Building
201 West 24th Street, 3rd
   Floor
New York, NY 10001

344 West Genesee
Syracuse, NY 13202

NEVADA

3085 South Valley View
   Boulevard
Las Vegas, NV 89102

350 South Rock Boulevard,
   Unit "B"
Reno, NV 89502

NORTH CAROLINA

Highland Park Commerce
   Center
810 Tyvola Road, Suite 132
Charlotte, NC 28217

OHIO

100 East Eighth Street
Cincinnati, OH 45202

Anthony J. Celebreeze
   Federal Building
1240 East Ninth Street
Cleveland, OH 44199

OKLAHOMA

West Park Business Center
4149 Highline Boulevard
Suite 300
Oklahoma City, OK 73108

OREGON

AT&T Building
202 S.E. Dorion Street
Pendleton, OR 97801

Federal Building
511 N.W. Broadway
Portland, OR 97209

PENNSYLVANIA

Fair Acres Center
Route 352
Lima, PA 19037

Moorehead Federal Building
1000 Liberty Avenue
Third Floor—Room 314
Pittsburgh, PA 15222

PUERTO RICO

1609 Ponce De Leon
Santurce, PR 00908

TENNESSEE

814 Federal Building
167 North Main Street
Memphis, TN 38103

TEXAS

2001 E. Division
Arlington, TX 76011

2800 South Interstate 25
Suite 115
Austin, TX 78704

Commerce 2
4410 Dillon Lane
Corpus Christi, TX 78415

7028 Alameda Ave.
Lakeside Shopping Center
El Paso, TX 79915

603 Ed Carey Drive
Harlingen, TX 78550

2974 Fulton
Houston, TX 77009

2331 Saunders Plaza
Laredo, TX 78043

1940 Avenue G
Lubbock, TX 79404

Alta Vista Retail Center
1007 Poteet Jourdanton
    Freeway
San Antonio, TX 78224

UTAH

2990 South Main Street
Salt Lake City, UT 84115

VERMONT

Federal Building
P.O. Box 328
St. Albans, VT 05478

VIRGINIA

1521 North Danville Street,
    1st Floor
Arlington, VA 22201

WASHINGTON

815 Airport Way South
Seattle, WA 98134

Franklin Building
1139 Princeton Street
Wenatchu, WA 98801

INS Building
315 North Fifth Avenue
Yakima, WA 98902

WISCONSIN

Federal Building
517 East Wisconsin Avenue
Milwaukee, WI 53202

How to Apply for Naturalization

If you are applying for citizenship, you will be tested on your knowledge of the government of the United States and its history. You will also be tested on your ability to read, write, and speak English, unless you have been living in the United States for a total of at least 20 years and were over 50 years old as of December 24, 1952, or unless you are physically unable to read, write, or speak.

GENERAL NATURALIZATION REQUIREMENTS

Every applicant must meet every requirement for naturalization, unless he or she is a person who comes within a special class that is exempt from some of those requirements. Check with the nearest office of the Immigration and Naturalization Service in your area to find which class you belong to.

FILING THE APPLICATION

The first step is to get an application form and, except for children under 14 years of age, a fingerprint card and a biographic information form from the nearest office of the Immigration and Naturalization Service. You can call by telephone and receive these papers by mail.

If you are applying for your own naturalization, the application form to be used is Form N-400, "Application to File Petition for Naturalization." If, however, a parent wants to file a petition for the naturalization of a child or an adopted child, the application to be used is Form N-402, "Application to File Petition of Naturalization in Behalf of Child."

The application, the fingerprint card, and the biographic information forms are furnished without charge. They must be filled out according to the instructions printed on them, and taken or mailed to the nearest office of Immigration and Naturalization Service. Along with the forms you must submit three photographs as described in the application.

EXAMINATION OF THE APPLICATION

After processing the application, the Immigration and Naturalization Service will inform you they have arranged an appointment with an examiner to discuss your application. The examiner will help you file the legal papers—known as "Petition for Naturalization"—in the Naturalization Court.

FINAL COURT HEARING

After the examination has been completed and the petition has been filed, you must wait for at least 30 days before you can have a final hearing in the Naturalization Court. Often the judge does not ask questions. However, it is wise to be on the safe side and be prepared to answer the questions you have been told you will be asked. When no questions are asked, the Naturalization Examiner informs the judge that you have been found qualified for naturalization and should be made a citizen.

When the court decides that you are eligible to become a citizen, you must take an Oath of Allegiance to the United States. In doing so, you give up allegiance to your former country and promise to support and defend the Constitution and laws of the United States.

SOME ADVICE TO REMEMBER WHEN YOU COME BEFORE THE EXAMINER OR COURT

Never be late for your appointment. If you are even a few minutes late for the examination of your application, you will be turned back, and a new date for the examination will be sent to you by mail.

If you are a man, wear a coat and tie; if you are a woman, wear a dress. DO NOT WEAR JEANS! Dress up for the occasion if you can.

Remember, always give your alien registration number when communicating with this service, and bring your card with you to the court hearing. You must turn it in to one of the examiners before you receive your Certificate of Naturalization. Lists of offices of the Immigration and Naturalization Service from which information may be obtained can be found in your local telephone directory under *United States Government*. If you cannot find the proper listing, dial Information.

The English and Citizenship Test

The INS offers a written alternative to the oral test of English, history, and government that is part of the INS interview for permanent residence and naturalization. This test consists of 20 multiple-choice questions on U.S. government history and one short English sentence read aloud which the candidate must then write or print in English.

You may sign up for two test sessions for a fee of $10. Each session lasts approximately 30 minutes. To pass the test, you must answer 12 out of 20 questions correctly in one session or 20 out of 40 questions correctly in the two sessions; you must also pass the writing exercise at this time.

The INS is notified if you pass the test. This means that you will not be asked any questions on English, government, or history at your INS interview. (The INS only receives the names of candidates who pass the exam; if you fail the exam, the INS is *not* notified.) You will receive an official notice confirming that you passed; be sure to bring this notification to your INS interview.

If you fail the exam after the first two sessions, you may try again the following month by signing up and paying the $10 fee. To prepare for the test, study the history and government sections of this book, as well as the Federal Textbooks on Citizenship. Some examples of the type of sentence you will be asked to write are found on page 37. The following are some sample test questions.

1. Who was the first president of the United States?

    A. Abraham Lincoln
    B. Thomas Jefferson
    C. James Madison
    D. George Washington

2. The United States Capitol is in

    A. Boston, MA
    B. Washington, DC
    C. New York City
    D. Los Angeles, CA

3. July 4 is

    A. Independence Day
    B. Memorial Day
    C. Veterans Day
    D. Presidents Day

Answers: 1. D   2. B   3. A

For further information on the English and Citizenship Test, call the National Association of Latino Elected and Appointed Officials (NALEO) hotline at 1–800–446-2536 (in California, call 1–800–346-2536).

History of the United States

Europeans came to America soon after its discovery. The Spanish began exploring Mexico, Central America, and parts of North America as early as 1510. Ponce de León landed on the east coast of Florida a few years later.

England sent a number of expeditions to explore the new world, largely on the east coast of North America. One man, Sir Walter Raleigh, led several expeditions and named the land he explored "Virginia," in honor of Elizabeth I, the Virgin Queen. But it was after the death of Elizabeth that a full-scale effort to establish English colonies in the New World began. This effort came from merchants—not from the new king, James I.

The first large group of settlers to leave England came here in 1620 for religious reasons. About 100 people set out from Plymouth, England, on a ship named the *Mayflower*. The ship landed in America in Cape Cod Bay. The settlers decided to remain, and claimed to be free of English law. Before going ashore, the Pilgrims drew up what they called the Mayflower Compact:

> We whose names are underwritten, do by these present, solemnly and mutually in the presence of God and one another covenant and combine ourselves under . . . into a civil body politic . . . and by virtue hereof do enact . . . such just and equal laws . . . as shall be thought must meet and convene for the general good of the colony.

This group of religious dissenters had, in their simple way, created a new government, with no laws controlling religious beliefs. In 1791 this declaration of freedom from religious persecution became part of the Constitution of the United States. English merchants continued to encourage emigration to the New World, and between 1660 and 1760 England had established 13 colonies in North America.

Settlers from other nations arrived—French, Irish, German, Dutch, and many others. With them came new cultures and lifestyles. These people became the first Americans.

During this period of colonization, between 1660 and 1760, most colonists continued to look to England for leadership. The northern colonies (Pennsylvania, New York, and New England) became more commercially inclined, while the South remained agricultural. Farming was hard and expensive. This and other problems with white labor contributed to the shift toward the use of slaves. By 1740, there were about 150,000 slaves in the South.

Meanwhile, the thirteen colonies were growing and the people were, to a large extent, independent from the king. During this time, Europe was continually at war and many immigrants came here to avoid being drafted. But there was little fighting in the New World until 1752, when the French and English clashed. The governor of Virginia appointed a young man by the name of George Washington to the rank of Lieutenant Colonel, to fight the French. Peace came in 1763, and the French abandoned their claims to North America except for two small islands in the St. Lawrence River. Canada became another of England's possessions at this time.

Because of the need for more revenue, England now began to tighten its control in the colonies. The continuing warring on the Continent as well as the war to drive the French out of America and Canada had been expensive, and the colonies were expected to help the economy by paying more taxes. Trouble broke out between the colonists and the British Army. Some Americans sought independence from England. In June 1774, Massachusetts called for the first meeting of delegates from the 13 colonies to take action. They agreed, and in September, the First Continental Congress met in Philadelphia, with only Georgia absent.

The Revolutionary War

In January 1775, England ordered armed troops to fire upon the citizens who were in revolt in Massachusetts. That incident is called "The Shot Heard Round the World." This armed action by England quickly rallied the other colonies to the cause of freedom. The American Revolution had begun.

The Continental Congress named George Washington, who had served as commander in chief of the Virginia militia, to command the Continental forces. On July 4, 1776, with the help of Thomas Jefferson, Benjamin Franklin, John Adams, Roger Sherman, and Robert Livingston, the new Congress adopted the Declaration of Independence. In March 1781, the Articles of Confederation had been ratified, and in 1783 the signing of the Treaty of Paris officially ended the seven-year American Revolutionary War. The new country had won its independence from England. General George Washington was a national hero; he is now called "The Father of Our Country."

The new country struggled to establish a new government. England and Spain were still in control of the land beyond the 13 states, and the Indians threatened the peace. America was young and weak. The 13 states had problems with the economy; the national government was not able to pay its debts.

The founding fathers called for a convention to change the Articles of Confederation. They altered the loose confederation of the former 13 colonies into a federated form, with a national government holding many of the powers once controlled by the states. That required consent by all the states. The meeting took place in Philadelphia. Delaware ratified in December, 1787, North Carolina in November, 1789, and Rhode Island held out until May, 1790. The first election took place between January and February of 1789, with George Washington the unanimous choice as the first president of the United States. John Adams won the Vice-Presidency.

On April 30, 1789, Washington took the Oath of Office. The problems with France, England, and Spain continued until 1794. Finally, on June 24, 1795, George Washington submitted to the senate a treaty with England, worked out by Chief Justice John Jay. It is called Jay's Treaty. This improved relations with England and helped the new nation grow without fear of war.

Without this danger, the United States began to expand. The Mississippi was now opened and the West was also, with the Louisiana Purchase from France and the explorations of Lewis and Clark. Other explorations followed and brought back information about the size and resources of this new land. This was a period of expansion for the United

States; unfortunately, wars with Indian tribes resulted. In 1812, war was again declared between the United States and England over freedom of the seas. The war was ended by the Treaty of Ghent in December 1814.

The country was again on the move towards prosperity, progress, and expansion. (See the chart of the Territorial Expansions, p. 28.) By 1820 the country had achieved major economic growth. In March 1836 Texas declared its independence from Mexico. In April, Sam Houston attacked the Mexican Army (lead by General Santa Anna) and drove the Mexican Army out of Texas. He was elected President of the Republic of Texas. However, Texas was to join the United States after a short period of being a separate nation.

War between the United States and Mexico was declared in 1846. As a result of the conflict, Mexico lost part of California and New Mexico. With expansion, the question of slavery came up once again, North and South opposing each other on the issue.

As the United States grew larger and richer, the North became more industrialized, while the South remained almost totally agricultural. Because of this, the South needed cheap labor and continued to depend on slaves.

The Civil War

In the election of 1860, Abraham Lincoln became the 16th President of the United States. Slavery concerned Lincoln deeply. His election caused the South to threaten to secede from the Union. Shortly after Lincoln's election, the South and the North declared war upon each other; the Civil War began in 1861 and ended in 1865. Slavery was officially abolished in the Confederate States of America by the Emancipation Proclamation (Jan. 1, 1863).

The 11 Southern states were brought back into the Union. Americans now had to forget war and try to reunite the country.

By 1893 the United States had become an industrial giant. Railroads, iron, oil, and electricity had changed the country into a great power and a world leader.

The Spanish-American War, 1898

Cuban rebels had been waging guerrilla warfare against Spain for many years. The United States wanted to oust the Spanish from Cuba, and in April 1898 Congress voted to recognize Cuba as an independent nation. American forces were sent to drive out the Spanish. Commodore George Dewey was ordered to move against the Spanish navy in the Philippine Islands (another Spanish possession); he defeated the Spanish fleet. Commodore Dewey asked for troops to be sent to hold Manila. In August, President William McKinley dispatched troops and Manila was captured. Meanwhile, Colonel Theodore Roosevelt was sent to Cuba; the Spanish surrendered on July 17. Puerto Rico and Guam, other Spanish possessions, became Territories of the United States. The Philippines were added, as well. In 1901, after a bitter fight between the United States and the Philippines, Congress allowed the islands to have their own civilian government. In July 1901 William Howard Taft became the first civilian Governor of the Philippines. In 1902 the United States pulled its troops out of Cuba, Puerto Rico, and Guam, but these countries remained United States Territories.

The Progressive Era

This period lasted from 1902 until America entered World War I. The Progressive Era was so called because of its relatively liberal outlook. The Seventeenth Amendment was adopted in 1913; this meant that United States Senators were no longer appointed but now elected by the people of each state.

Women were gaining support in their fight for the right to vote. However, this would not become a fact until 1920. The Anti-Trust Act was passed, making it illegal for large companies to band together and control one industry. Child labor laws were passed, and some protection was guaranteed workers in dangerous occupations. Public health became a legislative consideration, as well.

World War I—1914 to 1918

The United States had no wish to enter the war between Germany (and its allies) and France and Britain (and their allies). However, the sinking of the Lusitania in 1915 and the loss of freedom of the seas forced the United States into the war in 1917. Armistice was declared on November 11, 1918. The war had ended and the American people were ready to resume normal life.

Industrial output doubled from 1921 to 1929. But vast overextension of credit by the government and the public took its toll. On October 24, 1929, "Black Thursday," the stock market fell. This was the beginning of the Great Depression, which lasted from 1929 to 1939.

A New War Begins—World War II

When Germany invaded Poland in September 1939, Britain honored its treaty with Poland and declared war on Germany. There was little fighting during 1939. But in May of 1940, Germany altered events by first attacking Holland, Belgium, and Luxembourg, and then marching into France. In 1941 Germany invaded Russia. On December 7, 1941, the Japanese attacked Pearl Harbor, and war was declared on Japan and its allies by the United States. A peace treaty was signed in Europe in early 1945, but the war continued in the Pacific until the United States dropped its atom bomb on Hiroshima. Three days later, a second bomb hit Nagasaki. The Japanese surrendered on August 15, 1945. Following the end of World War II, the United States began, once again, to shift the economy from wartime back to peacetime.

Relations with America's former ally, Russia, gradually become strained. Historians call this unfriendly state of affairs the Cold War, due largely to Russia's and America's attempts to exert influence in the same areas. The economy thrived, unemployment was low, and business was booming. This boom in the economy and new peace was shattered in 1950 when North Koreans rumbled across the 38th parallel, which divided North and South Korea. American and United Nations troops fought the North Koreans until 1953. American troops remain in South Korea to this date.

Dwight D. Eisenhower became President in 1953. The economy was prosperous during the eight years Eisenhower was in office. One of the issues during his administration was civil rights; segregation in the Armed Forces was abolished at this time. But it was not until the Kennedy administration that stricter enforcement of civil rights became effective.

By August 1964, the United States was once again at war. In the early years of the Vietnamese War (from 1965 to 1967), about 165,000 American troops were fighting the Communists. By 1968, over 600,000 Americans were fighting. The war ended in January 1973. President Richard M. Nixon took credit for having ended the war.

The Nixon administration is a dark page in the history of the United States. During the investigation of the Watergate scandals, many officials called for his impeachment and resignation. His Vice President, Spiro T. Agnew, was accused of having accepted bribes when he was previously Governor of Maryland. Agnew resigned as Vice President and Nixon appointed Gerald R. Ford as Vice President, under the authority of the 25th Amendment. Meanwhile, the Watergate investigation continued. On August 8, 1974, Nixon announced his resignation. The next day, on August 9, 1974, Gerald Ford became the 38th President of the United States.

In the 1976 presidential elections, James (Jimmy) Carter defeated Gerald Ford and became the 39th president of the United States. Jimmy Carter was defeated in the 1980 elections by Ronald Reagan, who was succeeded by George Bush in 1988.

The United States faces many challenges at home and abroad in the coming decade, but there is hope that this country will continue to grow, develop, and change for the better.

(Note: The reader must remember that this short history is designed to meet the requirements for persons seeking to pass the necessary tests to become naturalized citizens of the United States. It is not meant to replace textbooks used in school.)

United States Government

Federal, State, and Local

The Constitution of the United States is called the "highest law of the land." It gives power to the Federal and state governments, and protects the rights of citizens. There are three branches to the Federal government: executive, judicial, and legislative.

Like the Federal government, each state has three branches: executive, judicial, and legislative. However, the governmental systems of the individual states are not all the same, because each state has its own constitution.

In state government the Governor, Lieutenant Governor, Secretary of State, Attorney General, and other officials are the executive branch. The Governor, like the President, has his duties which are spelled out in each state constitution.

The judicial system is unique in every state. Most, however, have a Supreme Court and a Court of Criminal Appeals. Their decisions can be overruled by the Federal courts and the United States Supreme Court.

The legislative branch of government in a state may also be unique with regard to structure, size, and power. The laws are created by the State Legislature, but when doubts arise about a new law or the authority of the state's local government, the courts decide whether they conflict with the United States Constitution. State legislators deal mostly with local matters affecting the cities.

A Mayor and a City Council are found in most cities. The City Council is a single chamber and its size can vary. Some City Councils have two members, others have as many as 50 or more. They are elected by popular vote.

American History

Questions and Answers

1. *Q.* Name the 13 original colonies.
   A. 1. Connecticut
   2. Delaware
   3. Georgia
   4. Maryland
   5. Massachusetts
   6. New Hampshire
   7. New Jersey
   8. New York
   9. North Carolina
   10. Pennsylvania
   11. Rhode Island
   12. South Carolina
   13. Virginia

2. *Q.* Who is called the "Father" of this country?
   A. George Washington

3. *Q.* Who was the commander-in-chief of the American Army at the time of the Revolutionary War?
   A. George Washington.

4. *Q.* What do the stripes of the United States flag stand for?
   A. The original 13 states.

5. *Q.* What are the highest mountains in the United States?
   A. The Rocky Mountains.

6. *Q.* Name the original 13 states.
   A. 1. Connecticut
   2. Delaware
   3. Georgia
   4. Maryland
   5. Massachusetts
   6. New Hampshire

7. New Jersey
8. New York
9. North Carolina
10. Pennsylvania
11. Rhode Island
12. South Carolina
13. Virginia

7. *Q.* Who was George Washington?
A. He was the Commander-in-Chief of the American Army at the time of the Revolutionary War. He was also the first President of the United States.

8. *Q.* Who was Abraham Lincoln?
A. He was the 16th President of the United States. He freed the slaves and saved the Union.

9. *Q.* What is the Declaration of Independence?
A. It is a document signed by the delegates from the 13 colonies on July 4, 1776, declaring that they were free and independent from Britain.

10. *Q.* What was the Revolutionary War?
A. It was the war between the 13 colonies and Britain over taxes and freedom. The colonies won the war.

11. *Q.* When was the Revolutionary War?
A. From 1775 to 1783.

12. *Q.* What was the Civil War?
A. It was the war between the North and the South over slavery and economics. The North won the war.

13. *Q.* When was the Civil War?
A. From 1861 to 1865.

14. *Q.* What do the stars of the United States flag represent?
A. Each star represents a state.

15. *Q.* What is the name of the national anthem?
A. *The Star Spangled Banner.*

16. *Q.* What are the most important documents in the history of the United States?
    A. 1. The Declaration of Independence.
    2. The Articles of Confederation.
    3. The Constitution.
    4. The Emancipation Proclamation.

17. *Q.* Who were the Pilgrims?
    A. They were among the first settlers to come to this country seeking freedom of religion. They arrived in Massachusetts in 1620.

18. *Q.* Who wrote the Constitution?
    A. Delegates from the 13 colonies.

19. *Q.* What is the United States?
    A. It is a federated union of 50 states.

20. *Q.* What is the capital of the United States?
    A. Washington, D.C.

21. *Q.* How many states are there in the United States?
    A. There are 50 states.

22. *Q.* Where does the President live?
    A. He lives in the White House in Washington, D.C.

23. *Q.* Who was the first President of the United States?
    A. George Washington.

24. *Q.* Who was the 16th President of the United States?
    A. Abraham Lincoln.

25. *Q.* What is the longest river in the United States?
    A. It is the Mississippi River.

26. *Q.* How many stars are there in the United States flag?
    A. There are 50 stars.

27. *Q.* How many stripes are there in the United States flag?
    A. There are 13 stripes (7 red and 6 white).

28. *Q.* What is the 4th of July?
    A. It is Independence Day of the United States.

29. *Q.* Have you studied the United States Constitution?
    A. Yes, I have.

30. *Q.* What is the Constitution?
    A. It is the highest law of the United States.

31. *Q.* Do you know the meaning of the colors of the United States flag?
    A. Yes: red is for courage, white is for purity, and blue is for justice and truth.

32. *Q.* Who wrote *The Star Spangled Banner?*
    A. It was written in 1814 by Francis Scott Key, a Maryland lawyer, during the bombardment of Fort McHenry. It was adopted by Congress as the national anthem in 1931.

33. *Q.* Name the territorial expansions.

1. Louisiana Purchase	1803
2. Florida	1819
3. Texas	1845
4. Oregon	1846
5. Mexican Cession	1848
6. Gadsden Purchase	1853
7. Alaska	1867
8. Hawaii	1898
9. The Philippines	1898–1946
10. Puerto Rico	1898
11. Guam	1898
12. American Samoa	1900
13. Canal Zone	1904–1979
14. U.S. Virgin Islands	1917
15. Pacific Islands	1947
16. Trust Territory	1947

34. *Q.* Name the Presidents of the United States and give the years they were in office.

A. George Washington	1789–1797
John Adams	1797–1801
Thomas Jefferson	1801–1809
James Madison	1809–1817

James Monroe	1817–1825
John Quincy Adams	1825–1829
Andrew Jackson	1829–1837
Martin Van Buren	1837–1841
William Henry Harrison	1841
John Tyler	1841–1845
James Knox Polk	1845–1849
Zachary Taylor	1849–1850
Millard Fillmore	1850–1853
Franklin Pierce	1853–1857
James Buchanan	1857–1861
Abraham Lincoln	1861–1865
Andrew Johnson	1865–1869
Ulysses Simpson Grant	1869–1877
Rutherford Birchard Hayes	1877–1881
James Abram Garfield	1881
Chester Alan Arthur	1881–1885
Grover Cleveland	1885–1889
Benjamin Harrison	1889–1893
Grover Cleveland	1893–1897
William McKinley	1897–1901
Theodore Roosevelt	1901–1909
William Howard Taft	1909–1913
Woodrow Wilson	1913–1921
Warren Gamaliel Harding	1921–1923
Calvin Coolidge	1923–1929
Herbert Clark Hoover	1929–1933
Franklin Delano Roosevelt	1933–1945
Harry S Truman	1945–1953
Dwight David Eisenhower	1953–1961
John Fitzgerald Kennedy	1961–1963
Lyndon Baines Johnson	1963–1969
Richard Milhous Nixon	1969–1974
Gerald Rudolph Ford (appointed)	1974–1977
James Earl Carter	1977–1981
Ronald Wilson Reagan	1981–1989
George Herbert Walker Bush	1989–

American Government

Questions and Answers

1. *Q.* How does the Government get the money needed to carry on its affairs?
   A. By taxation.

2. *Q.* Who levies the taxes?
   A. Congress.

3. *Q.* Where is the original document of the Constitution located?
   A. In the National Archives, in Washington, D.C.

4. *Q.* Do you know the names of the first three Presidents?
   A. Yes: George Washington, John Adams, and Thomas Jefferson.

5. *Q.* Who wrote the pledge to the flag of the United States (Pledge of Allegiance)?
   A. Francis Bellamy.

6. *Q.* Who elects the President?
   A. The people, through the Electoral College.

7. *Q.* In what state are you now living?
   A. In _____ (*give the name of your state*).

8. *Q.* Who makes the laws in your state?
   A. The State Legislature.

9. *Q.* Did we have a government before the Constitution?
   A. Yes, we had a government under the Articles of Confederation.

10. *Q.* What is the 22nd Amendment?
    A. The President can serve only two terms.

11. *Q.* What are the divisions of Congress?
    A. The Senate and the House of Representatives.

12. *Q.* What body advises the President in making policy decisions?
    A. A cabinet made up of eleven members.

13. *Q.* Can the President make treaties with other nations?
    A. Yes, he can make treaties with the consent of the Senate.

14. *Q.* What is the 26th Amendment?
    A. That a person 18 years of age or older can vote.

15. *Q.* What do you pledge when you stand before the national flag?
    A. *I pledge allegiance to the flag of the United States of America, and to the Republic for which it stands; one nation under God, indivisible, with liberty and justice for all.*

16. *Q.* How does an amendment become part of the Constitution?
    A. It is passed by Congress with a two-thirds vote and by a three-fourths vote in the State Legislatures.

17. *Q.* What is your nationality?
    A. *(Give correct answer.)*

18. *Q.* In order, name the successors to the President in case the President resigns or dies.
    A. 1. The Vice President
        2. The Speaker of the House.
        3. The President *pro tempore* of the Senate.

19. *Q.* What does impeachment mean?
    A. It means officially accusing an officer of wrongdoing and forcing that official to resign.

20. *Q.* How long does a Federal judge serve?
    A. For life, unless he or she is charged with unbecoming conduct.

21. *Q.* What is the 20th Amendment?
    A. It changed the date of the President's inauguration to January 20 and the opening date of Congress to January 3.

22. *Q.* (a) What is the Legislative Branch of the United States government?
    A.   The Congress.

    Q. (b) What is the Executive Branch?
    A.   The President and his Cabinet.

    Q. (c) What is the Judicial Branch?
    A.   The courts.

23. *Q.* Can Congress pass a bill in spite of the President's veto?
    A. Yes, by a two-thirds majority of Congress.

24. *Q.* Who appoints the justices of the Supreme Court?
    A. The President, with the consent of the Senate.

25. *Q.* What are the qualifications for Vice President?
    A. The same as for the President.

26. *Q.* What are the principles of the United States Constitution?
    A. Liberty, equality, and justice.

27. *Q.* What are the first ten Amendments called?
    A. The Bill of Rights.

28. *Q.* What is a democratic government?
    A. Government by the people through their elected representatives.

29. *Q.* What are the qualifications for United States Senator?
    A. A Senator must be an American citizen, 30 years old

1- What are the colors of our Flag?
Red, White, and Blue
2- How many stars are there in our
Flag? 50
3- What color are the stars on our
Flag? White
4- What do the stars on the Flag
mean? One for each state in
the union
5- How many stripes are there in the
Flag? 13
6- What color are the stripes? Red
and white
7- What do the stripes on the Flag
mean? They represent the original
13 states
8- How many states are there in the
union? 50
9- What is the 4th of July? Independence day
10- What is the date of independence
day? July 4th
11- Independence from Whom? England
12- What country did we fight during
the revolutionary war? England
13- Who was the frist president of
the United States? George Washington
14- Who is the president of the united
States today? Bill Clinton

15- Who is the Vice-president of the United States today? Al Gore
16- Who Elects the President of the United States? The Electoral College
17- Who Becomes President of the united ted States if the president should Die? Vice-President
18- For How Long Do we elect the president? Four Years
19- What is the constitution? The supreme Law of the Land
20- Can the constitution be changed? Yes
21- What Do we Call a Change to the constitution? AMendments
22- How many changes or Amendments are there to the constitution? 26
23- How many branches are there in our government? 3
24- What are the three branches of our government? Legislative, Executive, and Judiciary
25- What is the Legislative Branch of our Government? Congress
26- Who makes the laws in the — united States? Congress
27- What is Congress? The senate and the House of Representatives

28- What are the duties of congress?
   to make Laws

29- Who elects congress? The people

30- How many senators are there
   in congress? 100

31- Can you name the two senators
   from your state? McCain —
   De Concini

32- For How long do we elect each
   ch senator? 6 years

33- How many representatives are there
   in congress? 435

34- For how long do we elect the re
   presentatives? 2 years

35- What is the Executive Branch of
   our government? The President,
   Cabinet, and Departments under
   the cabinet members

36- What is the Judiciary Branch of
   our government? The Supreme Court

37- What are the duties of the Supre
   me Court? To interpret the Laws

38- What is the supreme Law of the
   united States? The Constitution

39- What is the Bill of Rights? The
   First 10 Amendments of the cons
   titution

40- What is the Capital of your state?
   Phoenix

51- Acording to the constitution, a person must meet certain requirements in order to Be eligible to become president, Name one of these requirements. Must be a natural citizen of the U.S.A.

52- Why are there 100 senators in the senate? two from each state

53- Who select the supreme cort Justice? Appointed by the president

54- How many supreme court are there? Nine (9)

55- Why did the pilgrims came to America? From religious freedom

56- What is the head executive of a state Government called? Governor

57- What is the head executive of a city Government called? Mayor

58- What holiday was celebrated for the first time by the American colonist? Thanksgiving

59- Who was the main writer of the declaration of independence? Thomas Jefferson

60- When was the declaration of independence adopted? July 4th 1776

61- What is the basic belief of the declaration of independence? that all men are created equal

83- Where does congress meet? In the capitol in Washington, D.C.

84- Whose rights are guaranteed - by the constitution and the Bill of rights? Everyone (Citizens and non-citizens living in the U.S.A.)

85- What is the introduction to the - constitution called? The Preamble

86- Name one benefit of being a citizen of the U.S.A.? Obtain federal Jobs; travel with A. U.S. Passport; Petition for close relatives to come to the U.S. to live.

87- What is the most important right granted to U.S. citizens? The right to vote

88- What is the United States Capitol? The place where congress meets

89- What is the White House? The president official home

90- Where is the White House Located? Washington, D.C. (1600 Pennsylvania Ave. N.W.)

91- What is the name of the president's official Home?
The White House

92- Name the ~~its~~ one right guaranteed by the first amendment?
Freedom to speech, Press, Religion

62- What is the national anthem of the united states? The Star-Spangled banner

63- Who wrote the star-Spangled Banner? Francis Scott Key

64- Where does freedom of speech — came from? The Bill of rights

65- What is the minimum voting age in the U.S.A.? 18

66- Who signs Bills into Laws? the President

67- What is the Highest court in the united States? The Supreme Court

68- Who was president during the civil war? Abraham Lincoln

69- What did the emancipation proclamation do? Freed many slaves

70- What special group advises the president? The Cabinet

71- Which President is called the father of our country? George Washington

72- What immigration and naturalization service form is used to apply to ~~become~~ become a Naturalized Citizen? From N-400 — "Aplication to file petition for Naturalization"

73- Who helped the pilgrims in America? The American Indians (Native Americans)

74- What is the name of the ship that brought the pilgrims to America? The Mayflower

75- What were the 13 original states of the union united States called? Colonies

76- Name 3 rights or freedoms guaranteed by the Bill of Rights?
1- The Right of freedom of Speech, Press, Religion, peaceable assembly and requesting change of Government.

77- Who has the power to declare war? The congress

78- What kind of government does the united States have? Republican

79- Which president freed the slaves? Abraham Lincoln

80- In what year was the constitution written? 1787

81- What are the First 10 Amendments to the constitution called? The Bill of rights

82- Name one purpose of the united nation? For countries to discuss and resolve problems, to provide economic aid to many countries

93- Who is the commander in Chief of the U.S. Military? The President
94- Which president was the first commander in Chief of the U.S. Military? George Washington
95- In what month is the do we vote for the president? November
96- In What month is the president inaugurated? January
97- How many times may Senator be re-elected? There is no Limit
98- How many times may congressman be re-elected? There is no limit
99- What are the 2 major Political parties in the U.S. Today? Democratic and Republican
100- How many states are there in the united States? Fifty (50)

or more. He or she must have lived in the United States for more than nine (9) years as an American citizen.

30. *Q.* What are the qualifications for United States Representative (Congressman)?
    A. A Representative must be an American citizen, 25 years old or more, who has lived in the United States for more than seven (7) years as an American citizen.

31. *Q.* What is meant by a Presidential veto?
    A. It is the President's refusal to sign a bill which has been passed by Congress.

32. *Q.* Is the American government a federation or centralized?
    A. It is a federation.

33. *Q.* Who makes the laws for each of the 50 states?
    A. The state legislature of each state.

34. *Q.* Who is the head of the Supreme Court?
    A. The Chief Justice.

35. *Q.* What are the major political parties in the United States?
    A. The Democratic party and the Republican party.

36. *Q.* Has any President been impeached?
    A. Yes. Andrew Johnson was impeached in 1868, but he was not convicted.

37. *Q.* Who is the head of the Armed Forces?
    A. The President.

38. *Q.* Can the President declare war?
    A. No.

39. *Q.* Can any state make a treaty or alliance with a foreign country?
    A. No, only the Federal Government can do so.

40. *Q.* What is the 16th Amendment?
    A. It allows the government to tax incomes.

41. *Q.* What is the 19th Amendment?
    A. It gives women the right to vote.

42. *Q.* How many Senators are there in Congress?
    A. There are 100.

43. *Q.* How many Amendments are there to the United States Constitution?
    A. There are 26 Amendments.

44. *Q.* What are the qualifications for President?
    A. The President must be over 35 years of age and a native-born citizen, who has lived in the United States for more than 14 years.

45. *Q.* Is the United States a dictatorship, a monarchy, or a republic?
    A. The United States is a republic.

46. *Q.* How many Representatives does each state have?
    A. The number depends on the population of each state.

47. *Q.* How many Senators does each state have?
    A. Each state has two (2) Senators.

48. *Q.* Who is the President of the United States at present?
    A. *(Give correct name of person now holding office.)*

49. *Q.* Who is the Vice President of the United States?
    A. *(Give correct name of person now holding office.)*

50. *Q.* Do you know the current population of the United States?
    A. Around 200 million.

51. *Q.* How long is a term in office for the President?
    A. Four years.

52. *Q.* How long is the term for a Senator?
    A. Six years.

53. *Q.* How long is the term for a Representative?
    A. Two years.

54. *Q.* What is an Amendment?
    A. It is a change or an addition to the Constitution.

55. *Q.* Who makes the laws of the United States?
    A. The Congress.

56. *Q.* If the President dies or cannot perform his duties, who takes his place?
    A. The Vice President.

57. *Q.* What are the three United States courts?
    A. 1. The United States Supreme Court.
       2. The United States Circuit Court.
       3. The United States District Court.

58. *Q.* What is the highest court in the United States?
    A. It is the United States Supreme Court.

59. *Q.* How many justices are there in the United States Supreme Court?
    A. There are nine justices.

60. *Q.* What are the three branches of the United States government?
    A. 1. Legislative
       2. Executive
       3. Judicial

61. *Q.* How are the State Representatives selected?
    A. They are elected by registered voters within each state.

62. *Q.* Who is the Governor of your state?
    A. *(Give correct name of person now holding office.)*

63. *Q.* Name one Congressman and one Senator from your state.
    A. *(Give correct names of the people holding these offices.)*

64. *Q.* When was your state admitted to the Union?
    A. *(Give correct date for the state in which you live.)*

65. *Q.* Where is the United States Supreme Court located?
    A. In Washington, D.C.

66. *Q.* What is the Cabinet?
    A. It is a group of people selected by the President and approved by the Senate who assist the President in special areas such as agriculture, commerce, foreign affairs, etc.

67. *Q.* Do you know the name of the bird that is the symbol of the United States?
    A. Yes, the bald eagle.

68. *Q.* What were the Articles of Confederation?
    A. They were the first Constitution of the United States.

69. *Q.* Who is Chief Executive of the United States?
    A. The President.

70. *Q.* Who said the following famous words? "Government of the people, by the people, for the people."
    A. Abraham Lincoln, in the Gettysburg Address (1863).

71. *Q.* Why were the Articles of Confederation discarded in favor of the present Constitution?
    A. Because Congress could make laws but could not enforce them, and there was no unity among the states.

72. *Q.* Can the residents of Washington, D.C., vote?
    A. Yes, in Federal elections and for mayor.

73. *Q.* What United States officials are elected by the people?
    A. The President, Vice President, Senators, and Representatives.

74. *Q.* Why do you want to become an American citizen?
    A. 1. *Example:* Because I am married to a person who is an American citizen.
    A. 2. *Example:* Because I like the freedom and democracy of the United States.

General Information

Sample Sentences

Write the following sentences, completing those which have blanks for answer choices.

1. I want to be an American citizen.

2. I have studied the American Constitution.

3. I have a pen in my right hand.

4. Today is a beautiful day.

5. This pen has _____ (*blue, black*) ink.

6. I went to a citizenship school for two months.

7. There are three colors in our flag: red, white, and blue.

8. There are fifty (50) states in the United States.

9. I came to _____ (*state*) from _____ (*country*) on _____ (*April 5th*) (*yesterday*) (*last week*).

10. I am wearing a _____ (*blue, red, green*) dress.

11. I am here to take my test today.

12. Yesterday was a _____ (*cold, warm, hot*) day.

13. I can read, write, and speak simple English.

14. There are many cars on the street.

15. I am working at _____.

16. I am wearing _____ (*yellow, brown, gray*) shoes.

17. It is raining now.

18. I have been married for _____ years.

19. We do not have any children (yet).

20. We have _____ children: _____ sons and _____ daughters.

21. We have _____ son(s).

22. My first name is _____.

23. I was married _____ years ago.

24. May I write something else?

25. I will do my best to be a worthy citizen.

26. I enjoy my work.

The Declaration of Independence

In Congress, July 4, 1776

The Unanimous Declaration of the Thirteen United States of America

When in the course of human events, it becomes necessary for one people to dissolve the political bands which have connected them with another, and to assume among the powers of the earth, the separate and equal station to which the laws of Nature and of Nature's God entitle them, a decent respect to the opinions of mankind requires that they should declare the causes which impel them to the separation.

We hold these truths to be self-evident, that all men are created equal, that they are endowed by their Creator with certain unalienable rights, that among these are life, liberty and the pursuit of happiness. That to secure these rights, governments are instituted among men, deriving their just powers from the consent of the governed,—That whenever any form of government becomes destructive of these ends, it is the right of the people to alter or to abolish it, and to institute new government, laying its foundation on such principles and organizing its powers in such form, as to them shall seem most likely to effect their safety and happiness. Prudence, indeed, will dictate that governments long established should not be changed for light and transient causes; and accordingly all experience hath shown, that man-kind are more disposed to suffer, while evils are sufferable, than to right themselves by abolishing the forms to which they are accustomed. But when a long train of abuses and usurpations, pursuing invariably the same object evinces a design to reduce them under absolute despotism, it is their right, it is their duty, to throw off such government, and to provide new guards for their future security.—Such has been the patient sufferance of these Colonies; and such is now the necessity which constrains them to alter their former systems of government. The history of the present King of Great Britain is a history of repeated injuries and usurpations, all having in direct object the establishment of an absolute tyranny over these States. To prove this, let facts be submitted to a candid world.

He has refused his assent to laws, the most wholesome and necessary for the public good.

He has forbidden his Governors to pass laws of immediate and pressing importance, unless suspended in their operation till his assent should be obtained; and when so suspended, he has utterly neglected to attend to them.

He has refused to pass other laws for the accommodation of large districts of people, unless those people would relinquish the right of representation in the legislature, a right inestimable to them and formidable to tyrants only.

He has called together legislative bodies at places unusual, uncomfortable, and distant from the depository of their public records, for the sole purpose of fatiguing them into compliance with his measures.

He has dissolved Representative Houses repeatedly, for opposing with manly firmness his invasions on the rights of the people.

He has refused for a long time, after such dissolutions, to cause others to be elected; whereby the legislative powers, incapable of annihilation, having returned to the people at large for their exercise; the State remaining in the mean time exposed to all the dangers of invasion from without, and convulsions within.

He has endeavoured to prevent the population of these States; for that purpose obstructing the laws for naturalization of foreigners; refusing to pass others to encourage their migrations hither, and raising the conditions of new appropriations of lands.

He has obstructed the administration of justice, by refusing his assent to laws for establishing judiciary powers.

He has made judges dependent on his will alone, for the

tenure of their offices, and the amount and payment of their salaries.

He has erected a multitude of new offices, and sent hither swarms of officers to harass our people, and eat out their substance.

He has kept among us, in times of peace, standing armies without the consent of our legislatures.

He has affected to render the military independent of and superior to the civil power.

He has combined with others to subject us to a jurisdiction foreign to our constitution, and unacknowledged by our laws; giving his assent to their acts of pretended legislation:

For quartering large bodies of armed troops among us:

For protecting them, by a mock trial, from punishment for any murders which they should commit on the inhabitants of these States:

For cutting off our trade with all parts of the world:

For imposing taxes on us without our consent:

For depriving us in many cases, of the benefits of trial by jury:

For transporting us beyond seas to be tried for pretended offenses:

For abolishing the free system of English laws in a neighbouring province, establishing therein an arbitrary government, and enlarging its boundaries so as to render it at once an example and fit instrument for introducing the same absolute rule into these colonies:

For taking away our charters, abolishing our most valuable laws, and altering fundamentally the forms of our governments:

For suspending our own legislatures, and declaring themselves invested with power to legislate for us in all cases whatsoever.

He has abdicated government here, by declaring us out of his protection and waging war against us.

He has plundered our seas, ravaged our coasts, burnt our towns, and destroyed the lives of our people.

He is at this time transporting large armies of foreign mercenaries to complete the works of death, desolation and tyranny, already begun with circumstances of cruelty and perfidy scarcely paralleled in the most barbarous ages, and totally unworthy the head of a civilized nation.

He has constrained our fellow citizens taken captive on the high seas to bear arms against their country, to become the executioners of their friends and brethren, or to fall themselves by their hands.

He has excited domestic insurrections amongst us, and has endeavoured to bring on the inhabitants of our frontiers, the merciless Indian savages, whose known rule of warfare is an undistinguished destruction of all ages, sexes and conditions.

In every stage of these oppressions we have petitioned for redress in the most humble terms: Our repeated petitions have been answered only by repeated injury. A prince, whose character is thus marked by every act which may define a tyrant, is unfit to be the ruler of a free people.

Nor have we been wanting in attentions to our British brethren. We have warned them from time to time of attempts by their legislature to extend an unwarrantable jurisdiction over us. We have reminded them of the circumstances of our emigration and settlement here. We have appealed to their native justice and magnanimity, and we have conjured them by the ties of our common kindred to disavow these usurpations, which would inevitably interrupt our connections and correspondence. They too have been deaf to the voice of justice and of consanguinity. We must, therefore, acquiesce in the necessity which denounces our separation, and hold them, as we hold the rest of mankind, enemies in war, in peace friends.

WE, THEREFORE, the Representatives of the United States of America, in General Congress, Assembled, appealing to the Supreme Judge of the world for the rectitude of our intentions, do, in the name, and by authority of the good people of these Colonies, solemnly publish and declare, That these United Colonies are, and of right ought to be FREE AND INDEPENDENT STATES; that they are absolved from all allegiance to the British Crown, and that all political connection between them and the State of Great Britain, is and ought to be totally dissolved; and that as free and independent States, they have full power to levy war, conclude peace, contract alliances, establish commerce, and to do all other acts and things which independent States may of right do. And for the support of this Declaration, with a firm reliance on the protection of Divine Providence, we mutually pledge to each other our lives, our fortunes and our sacred honor.

John Hancock.

New Hampshire

Josiah Bartlett
Wm. Whipple

Matthew Thornton

Massachusetts Bay

Saml. Adams
John Adams

Robt. Treat Paine
Elbridge Gerry

Rhode Island

Step. Hopkins

William Ellery

Connecticut

Roger Sherman
Saml. Huntington

Wm. Williams
Oliver Wolcott

New York

Wm. Floyd
Phil. Livingston

Frans. Lewis
Lewis Morris

New Jersey

Richd. Stockton
Jno. Witherspoon
Fras. Hopkinson

John Hart
Abra. Clark

Pennsylvania

Robt. Morris
Benjamin Rush
Benja. Franklin
John Morton
Geo. Clymer

Jas. Smith
Geo. Taylor
James Wilson
Geo. Ross

Delaware

Caesar Rodney
Geo. Read

Tho. M'Kean

Maryland

Samuel Chase
Wm. Paca
Thos. Stone

Charles Carroll
   of Carrollton

Virginia

George Wythe
Richard Henry Lee
Th. Jefferson
Benja. Harrison

Thos. Nelson Jr.
Francis Lightfoot Lee
Carter Braxton

North Carolina

Wm. Hooper
Joseph Hewes

John Penn

South Carolina

Edward Rutledge
Thos. Heyward Junr.

Thomas Lynch Junr.
Arthur Middleton

Georgia

Button Gwinnett
Lyman Hall

Geo. Walton

Constitution of the United States of America

PREAMBLE

WE THE PEOPLE of the United States, in order to form a more perfect Union, establish justice, insure domestic tranquility, provide for the common defense, promote the general welfare, and secure the blessings of liberty to ourselves and our posterity, do ordain and establish this Constitution for the United States of America.

ARTICLE I

SECTION 1. All legislative powers herein granted shall be vested in a Congress of the United States, which shall consist of a Senate and House of Representatives.

SECTION 2. The House of Representatives shall be composed of members chosen every second year by the people of the several States, and the electors in each State shall have the qualifications requisite for electors of the most numerous branch of the State Legislature.

No person shall be a representative who shall not have attained to the age of twenty-five years, and been seven years a citizen of the United States, and who shall not, when elected, be an inhabitant of that State in which he shall be chosen.

Representatives and direct taxes shall be apportioned among the several States which may be included within this Union, according to their respective numbers, which shall be determined by adding to the whole number of free persons, including those bound to service for a term of years, and excluding Indians not taxed, three-fifths of all other persons. The actual enumeration shall be made within three years after the first meeting of the Congress of the United States, and within every subsequent term of ten years, in such manner as they shall by law direct. The number of representatives shall not exceed one for every thirty thousand, but each State shall have at least one representative; and until such enumeration shall be made, the

State of New Hampshire shall be entitled to choose three, Massachusetts eight, Rhode Island and Providence Plantations one, Connecticut five, New York six, New Jersey four, Pennsylvania eight, Delaware one, Maryland six, Virginia ten, North Carolina five, South Carolina five, and Georgia three.

When vacancies happen in the representation from any State, the Executive authority thereof shall issue writs of election to fill such vacancies.

The House of Representatives shall choose their Speaker and other officers; and shall have the sole power of impeachment.

SECTION 3. The Senate of the United States shall be composed of two senators from each State, chosen by the legislature thereof, for six years and each senator shall have one vote.

Immediately after they shall be assembled in consequence of the first election, they shall be divided as equally as may be into three classes. The seats of the senators of the first class shall be vacated at the expiration of the second year, of the second class at the expiration of the fourth year, and of the third class at the expiration of the sixth year, so that one-third may be chosen every second year; and if vacancies happen by resignation, or otherwise, during the recess of the legislature of any State, the executive thereof may make temporary appointments until the next meeting of the legislature, which shall then fill such vacancies.

No person shall be a senator who shall not have attained to the age of thirty years, and been nine years a citizen of the United States, and who shall not, when elected, be an inhabitant of that State for which he shall be chosen.

The Vice President of the United States shall be President of the Senate, but shall have no vote, unless they be equally divided.

The Senate shall choose their other officers, and also a President pro tempore, in the absence of the Vice President, or when he shall exercise the office of President of the United States.

The Senate shall have the sole power to try all impeachments. When sitting for that purpose, they shall be on oath or affirmation. When the President of the United States is tried, the Chief Justice shall preside: And no person shall be convicted without the concurrence of two thirds of the members present.

Judgment in cases of impeachment shall not extend further

than to removal from office, and disqualification to hold and enjoy any office or honor, trust or profit under the United States; but the party convicted shall nevertheless be liable and subject to indictment, trial, judgment and punishment, according to law.

SECTION 4. The times, places and manner of holding elections for senators and representatives, shall be prescribed in each State by the legislature thereof; but the Congress may at any time by law make or alter such regulations, except as to the places of choosing senators.

The Congress shall assemble at least once in every year, and such meeting shall be on the first Monday in December, unless they shall by law appoint a different day.

SECTION 5. Each house shall be the judge of the elections, returns and qualifications of its own members, and a majority of each shall constitute a quorum to do business; but a smaller number may adjourn from day to day, and may be authorized to compel the attendance of absent members, in such manner, and under such penalties as each house may provide.

Each house may determine the rules of its proceedings, punish its members for disorderly behaviour, and, with the concurrence of two-thirds, expel a member.

Each house shall keep a journal of its proceedings, and from time to time publish the same, excepting such parts as may in their judgment require secrecy; and the yeas and the nays of the members of either house on any question shall, at the desire of one-fifth of those present, be entered on the journal.

Neither house, during the session of Congress, shall, without the consent of the other, adjourn for more than three days, nor to any other place than that in which the two houses shall be sitting.

SECTION 6. The senators and representatives shall receive a compensation for their services, to be ascertained by law, and paid out of the Treasury of the United States. They shall in all cases, except treason, felony and breach of the peace, be privileged from arrest during their attendance at the session of their respective houses, and in going to and returning from the same; and for any speech or debate in either house, they shall not be questioned in any other place.

No senator or representative shall, during the time for which he was elected, be appointed to any civil office under the authority of the United States, which shall have been created, or the emoluments whereof shall have been increased during such time; and no person holding any office under the United States, shall be a member of either house during his continuance in office.

SECTION 7. All bills for raising revenue shall originate in the House of Representatives; but the Senate may propose or concur with amendments as on other bills.

Every bill which shall have passed the House of Representatives and the Senate, shall, before it become a law, be presented to the President of the United States; if he approves he shall sign it, but if not he shall return it, with his objections to that house in which it shall have originated, who shall enter for the objections at large on their journal, and proceed to reconsider it. If after such reconsideration two thirds of that House shall agree to pass the bill, it shall be sent, together with the objections, to the other House, by which it shall likewise be reconsidered, and if approved by two thirds of that House, it shall become a law. But in all cases the votes of both Houses shall be determined by yeas and nays, and the names of the persons voting for and against the bill shall be entered on the journal of each House respectively. If any bill shall not be returned by the President within ten days (Sundays excepted) after it shall have been presented to him, the same shall be a law, in like manner as if he had signed it, unless the Congress by their adjournment prevent its return, in which case it shall not be a law.

Every order, resolution, or vote to which the concurrence of the Senate and House of Representatives may be necessary (except on a question of adjournment) shall be presented to the President of the United States; and before the same shall take effect, shall be approved by him, or being disapproved by him, shall be repassed by two thirds of the Senate and House of Representatives, according to the rules and limitations pre-scribed in the case of a bill.

SECTION 8. The Congress shall have power to lay and collect taxes, duties, imposts and excises, to pay the debts and provide for the common defense and general welfare of the United States; but all duties, imposts and excises shall be uniform throughout the United States;

To borrow money on the credit of the United States;

To regulate commerce with foreign nations, and among the several States, and with the Indian tribes;

To establish a uniform rule of naturalization, and uniform

laws on the subject of bankruptcies throughout the United States;

To coin money, regulate the value thereof, and of foreign coin, and fix the standard of weights and measures;

To provide for the punishment of counterfeiting the securities and current coin of the United States;

To establish post offices and post roads;

To promote the progress of science and useful arts, by securing for limited times to authors and inventors the exclusive right to their respective writings and discoveries;

To constitute tribunals inferior to the Supreme Court;

To define and punish piracies and felonies committed on the high seas, and offenses against the law of nations;

To declare war, grant letters of marque and reprisal, and make rules concerning captures on land and water;

To raise and support armies, but no appropriation of money to that use shall be for a longer term than two years;

To provide and maintain a Navy;

To make rules for the government and regulation of the land and naval forces;

To provide for calling forth the militia to execute the laws of the Union, suppress insurrections and repel invasions;

To provide for organizing, arming, and disciplining the militia, and for governing such part of them as may be employed in the service of the United States, reserving to the States respectively, the appointment of officers, and the authority of training the militia according to the discipline prescribed by Congress;

To exercise exclusive legislation in all cases whatsoever, over such district (not exceeding ten miles square) as may, by cession of particular States, and the acceptance of Congress, become the seat of the Government of the United States, and to exercise like authority over all places purchased by the consent of the legislature of the State in which the same shall be, for the erection of forts, magazines, arsenals, dock-yards, and other needful buildings;—And

To make all laws which shall be necessary and proper for carrying into execution the foregoing powers and all other powers vested by this Constitution in the Government of the United States, or in any department or officer thereof.

SECTION 9. The migration or importation of such persons as any of the States now existing shall think proper to admit, shall not be prohibited by the Congress prior to the year one thousand eight hundred and eight, but a tax or duty may be imposed on such importation, not exceeding ten dollars for each person.

The privilege of the writ of habeas corpus shall not be suspended, unless when in cases of rebellion or invasion the public safety may require it.

No bill of attainder or ex post facto law shall be passed.

No capitation, or other direct, tax shall be laid, unless in proportion to the census or enumeration herein before directed to be taken.

No tax or duty shall be laid on articles exported from any State.

No preference shall be given by any regulation of commerce revenue to the ports of one State over those of another: nor shall vessels bound to, or from, one State, be obliged to enter, clear, or pay duties in another.

No money shall be drawn from the Treasury, but in consequence of appropriations made by law; and a regular statement and account of the receipts and expenditures of all public money shall be published from time to time.

No title of nobility shall be granted by the United States: And no person holding any office of profit or trust under them, shall, without consent of the Congress, accept of any present, emolument, office, or title, of any kind whatever, from any King, Prince, or foreign State.

SECTION 10. No State shall enter into any treaty, alliance, or confederation, grant letters of marque and reprisal; coin money; emit bills of credit; make any thing but gold and silver coin a tender in payment of debts; pass any bill of attainder, ex post facto law, or law impairing the obligation of contracts, or grant any title of nobility.

No State shall, without the consent of the Congress, lay any imposts or duties on imports or exports, except what may be absolutely necessary for executing its inspection laws: and the net produce of all duties and imposts, laid by any State on imports or exports, shall be for the use of the Treasury of the United States; and all such laws shall be subject to the revision and control of the Congress.

No State shall, without the consent of Congress, lay any duty of tonnage, keep troops, or ships of war in time of peace, enter into any agreement or compact with another State, or with a foreign power, or engage in war, unless actually invaded, or in such imminent danger as will not admit of delay.

ARTICLE II

SECTION 1. The executive power shall be vested in a President of the United States of America. He shall hold his office during the term of four years, and, together with the Vice President, chosen for the same term, be elected, as follows:

Each State, shall appoint, in such manner as the legislature thereof may direct, a number of electors, equal to the whole number of senators and representatives to which the State may be entitled in the Congress; but no senator or representative, or person holding an office of trust or profit under the United States, shall be appointed an elector.

The electors shall meet in their respective States, and vote by ballot for two persons, of whom one at least shall not be an inhabitant of the same State with themselves. And they shall make a list of all the persons voted for, and of the number of votes for each; which list they shall sign and certify, and transmit sealed to the seat of the Government of the United States, directed to the President of the Senate. The President of the Senate shall, in the presence of the Senate and House of Representatives, open all the certificates, and the votes shall then be counted. The person having the greatest number of votes shall be the President, if such number be a majority of the whole number of electors appointed; and if there be more than one who have such majority, and have an equal number of votes, then the House of Representatives shall immediately choose by ballot one of them for President; and if no person have a majority, then from the five highest on the list the said House shall in like manner choose the President. But in choosing the President, the votes shall be taken by States, the representation from each State having one vote; a quorum for this purpose shall consist of a member or members from two thirds of the States, and a majority of all the States shall be necessary to a choice. In every case, after the choice of the President, the person having the greatest number of votes of the electors shall be the Vice President. But if there should remain two or more who have equal votes, the Senate shall choose from them by ballot the Vice President.

The Congress may determine the time of choosing the electors, and the day on which they shall give their votes; which day shall be the same throughout the United States.

No person except a natural born citizen, or a citizen of the United States, at the time of the adoption of this Constitution, shall be eligible to the office of President; neither shall any person be eligible to that office who shall not have attained to the age of thirty-five years, and been fourteen years a resident within the United States.

In case of the removal of the President from office, or of his death, resignation, or inability to discharge the powers and duties of the said office, the same shall devolve on the Vice President, and the Congress may by law provide for the case of removal, death, resignation, or inability, both of the President and Vice President, declaring what officer shall then act as President, and such officer shall act accordingly, until the disability be removed, or a President shall be elected.

The President shall, at stated times, receive for his services, a compensation, which shall neither be increased nor diminished during the period for which he shall have been elected, and he shall not receive within that period any other emolument from the United States, or any of them.

Before he enter on the execution of his office, he shall take the following oath or affirmation:—"I do solemnly swear (or affirm) that I will faithfully execute the office of President of the United States, and will to the best of my ability, preserve, protect and defend the Constitution of the United States."

SECTION 2. The President shall be Commander in Chief of the Army and Navy of the United States, and of the militia of the several States, when called into the actual service of the United States; he may require the opinion, in writing, of the principal officer in each of the Executive Departments, upon any subject relating to the duties of their respective offices, and he shall have power to grant reprieves and pardons for offenses against the United States, except in cases of impeachment.

He shall have power, by and with the advice and consent of the Senate, to make treaties, provided two-thirds of the Senators present concur; and he shall nominate, and by and with the advice and consent of the Senate, shall appoint ambassadors, other public ministers and consuls, Judges of the Supreme Court, and all other officers of the United States, whose appointments are not herein otherwise provided for, and which shall be established by law: but the Congress may by law vest the appointment of such inferior officers, as they think proper, in the President alone, in the courts of law, or in the heads of departments.

The President shall have power to fill up all vacancies that may happen during the recess of the Senate, by granting commissions which shall expire at the end of their next session.

SECTION 3. He shall from time to time give to the Congress information of the state of the Union, and recommend to their consideration such measures as he shall judge necessary and expedient; he may, on extraordinary occasions, convene both houses, or either of them, and in case of disagreement between them, with respect to the time of adjournment, he may adjourn them to such time as he shall think proper; he shall receive ambassadors and other public ministers; he shall take care that the laws be faithfully executed, and shall commission all the officers of the United States.

SECTION 4. The President, Vice President and all civil officers of the United States, shall be removed from office on impeachment for, and conviction of, treason, bribery, or other high crimes and misdemeanors.

ARTICLE III

SECTION 1. The judicial power of the United States, shall be vested in one Supreme Court, and in such inferior courts as the Congress may from time to time ordain and establish. The judges, both of the supreme and inferior courts, shall hold their offices during good behaviour, and shall, at stated times, receive for their services, a compensation, which shall not be diminished during their continuance of office.

SECTION 2. The judicial power shall extend to all cases, in law and equity, arising under this Constitution, the laws of the United States, and treaties made, or which shall be made, under their authority; to all cases affecting ambassadors, other public ministers and consuls; to all cases of admiralty and maritime jurisdiction; to controversies to which the United States shall be a party; to controversies between two or more States; between a State and citizens of another State; between citizens of different States; between citizens of the same State claiming lands under grants of different States, and between a State, or the citizens thereof, and foreign States, citizens or subjects.

In all cases affecting ambassadors, other public ministers and consuls, and those in which a State shall be a party, the Supreme Court shall have original jurisdiction. In all the other cases before mentioned, the Supreme Court shall have appellate jurisdiction, both as to law and fact, with such exceptions, and under such regulations as the Congress shall make.

The trial of all crimes, except in cases of impeachment, shall be by jury; and such trial shall be held in the State where the said crimes shall have been committed; but when not committed within any State, the trial shall be at such place or places as the Congress may by law have directed.

SECTION 3. Treason against the United States, shall consist only in levying war against them, or in adhering to their enemies, giving them aid and comfort. No person shall be convicted of treason unless on the testimony of two witnesses to the same overt act, or on confession in open court.

The Congress shall have power to declare the punishment of treason, but no attainder of treason shall work corruption of blood, or forfeiture except during the life of the person attained.

ARTICLE IV

SECTION 1. Full faith and credit shall be given in each State to the public acts, records, and judicial proceedings of every other State. And the Congress may by general laws prescribe the manner in which such acts, records and proceedings shall be proved, and the effect thereof.

SECTION 2. The citizens of each State shall be entitled to all privileges and immunities of citizens in the several States.

A person charged in any State with treason, felony, or other crime, who shall flee from justice, and be found in another State, shall on demand of the executive authority of the State from which he fled, be delivered up, to be removed to the State having jurisdiction of the crime.

No person held to service or labour in one State, under the laws thereof; escaping into another, shall, in consequence of any law or regulation therein, be discharged from such service or labour, but shall be delivered up on claim of the party to whom such service or labour may be due.

SECTION 3. New States may be admitted by the Congress into this Union; but no new State shall be formed or erected within the jurisdiction of any other State; nor any State be formed by the junction of two or more States, or parts of States, without the consent of the legislatures of the States concerned as well as of the Congress.

The Congress shall have power to dispose of and make all needful rules and regulations respecting the Territory or other property belonging to the United States; and nothing in this Constitution shall be so construed as to prejudice any claims of the United States, or of any particular State.

SECTION 4. The United States shall guarantee to every State in this Union a republican form of Government, and shall protect each of them against invasion; and on application of the legislature, or of the executive (when the legislature cannot be convened) against domestic violence.

ARTICLE V

The Congress, whenever two thirds of both Houses shall deem it necessary, shall propose amendments to this Constitution, or on the application of the legislatures of two thirds of the several States, shall call a convention for proposing amendments, which, in either case, shall be valid to all intents and purposes, as part of this Constitution, when ratified by the legislatures of three fourths of the several States, or by conventions in three fourths thereof, as the one or the other mode of ratification may be proposed by the Congress; provided that no amendment which may be made prior to the year one thousand eight hundred and eight shall in any manner affect the first and fourth clauses in the Ninth Section of the First Article; and that no State, without its consent, shall be deprived of its equal suffrage in the Senate.

ARTICLE VI

All debts contracted and engagements entered into, before the adoption of this Constitution, shall be as valid against the United States under this Constitution, as under the Confederation.

This Constitution, and the laws of the United States which shall be made in pursuance thereof; and all treaties made, or which shall be made, under the authority of the United States, shall be the supreme law of the land; and the judges in every State shall be bound thereby, any thing in the Constitution or laws of any State to the contrary notwithstanding.

The senators and representatives before mentioned, and the members of the several State legislatures, and all executive and judicial officers, both of the United States and of the several States, shall be bound by oath or affirmation, to support this Constitution; but no religious test shall ever be required as a qualification to any office or public trust under the United States.

ARTICLE VII

The ratification of the conventions of nine States shall be sufficient for the establishment of this Constitution between the States so ratifying the same.

Done in convention by the unanimous consent of the States present the seventeenth day of September in the year of our Lord one thousand seven hundred and eighty seven and of the Independence of the United States of America the twelfth. In witness whereof we have hereunto subscribed our names,

Go. Washington—*Presid't.*
and deputy from Virginia

Attest William Jackson—*Secretary*

New Hampshire

John Langdon   Nicholas Gilman

Massachusetts

Nathaniel Gorham   Rufus King

Connecticut

Wm. Saml. Johnson   Roger Sherman

New York

Alexander Hamilton

New Jersey

Wil: Livingston   Wm. Paterson
David Brearley   Jona: Dayton

Pennsylvania

B. Franklin

Thomas Mifflin

Robt. Morris

Geo. Clymer

Thos. FitzSimons

Jared Ingersoll

James Wilson

Gouv. Morris

Delaware

Geo: Read

Gunning Bedford Jun

John Dickinson

Richard Bassett

Jaco: Broom

Maryland

James McHenry

Dan. of St. Thos. Jenifer

Danl. Carroll

Virginia

John Blair

James Madison, Jr.

North Carolina

Wm. Blount

Richd. Dobbs Spaight

Hu. Williamson

South Carolina

J. Rutledge

Charles Cotesworth Pinckney

Charles Pinckney

Pierce Butler

Georgia

William Few

Abr. Baldwin

Amendments

ARTICLE I

Congress shall make no law respecting an establishment of religion, or prohibiting the free exercise thereof; or abridging the freedom of speech, or of the press; or the right of the people peaceably to assemble, and to petition the Government for a redress of grievances.

ARTICLE II

A well regulated militia, being necessary to the security of a free State, the right of the people to keep and bear arms, shall not be infringed.

ARTICLE III

No soldier shall, in time of peace be quartered in any house, without the consent of the owner, nor in time of war, but in a manner to be prescribed by law.

ARTICLE IV

The right of the people to be secure in their persons, houses, papers, and effects, against unreasonable searches and seizures, shall not be violated, and no warrants shall issue, but upon probable cause, supported by oath or affirmation, and particularly describing the place to be searched, and the persons or things to be seized.

ARTICLE V

No person shall be held to answer for a capital, or otherwise infamous crime, unless on a presentment or indictment of a Grand Jury, except in cases arising in the land or naval forces, or in the militia, when in actual service in time of war or public danger; nor shall any person be subject for the same offense to be twice put in jeopardy of life or limb; nor shall be compelled in any criminal case to be a witness against himself, nor be deprived of life, liberty, or property, without due process of law; nor shall private property be taken for public use, without just compensation.

ARTICLE VI

In all criminal prosecutions, the accused shall enjoy the right to a speedy and public trial, by an impartial jury of the State and district wherein the crime shall have been committed, which district shall have been previously ascertained by law, and to be informed of the nature and cause of the accusation; to be confronted with the witnesses against him; to have compulsory process for obtaining witnesses in his favor, and to have the assistance of counsel for his defense.

ARTICLE VII

In suits at common law, where the value in controversy shall exceed twenty dollars, the right of trial by jury shall be preserved, and no fact tried by a jury, shall be otherwise reexamined in any court of the United States, than according to the rules of the common law.

ARTICLE VIII

Excessive bail shall not be required, nor excessive fines imposed, nor cruel and unusual punishments inflicted.

ARTICLE IX

The enumeration in the Constitution, of certain rights, shall not be construed to deny or disparage others retained by the people.

ARTICLE X

The powers not delegated to the United States by the Constitution, nor prohibited by it to the States, are reserved to the States respectively, or to the people.

ARTICLE XI

The judicial power of the United States shall not be construed to extend to any suit in law or equity, commenced or prosecuted against one of the United States by citizens of another State, or by citizens or subjects of any foreign State.

ARTICLE XII

The electors shall meet in their respective States, and vote by ballot for President and Vice President, one of whom, at least, shall not be an inhabitant of the same State with themselves; they shall name in their ballots the person voted for as President, and in distinct ballots the person voted for as Vice President, and they shall make distinct lists of all persons voted for as President, and of all persons voted for as Vice President, and of the number of votes for each, which lists they shall sign and certify, and transmit sealed to the seat of the government of the United States, directed to the President of the Senate;—The President of the Senate shall, in the presence of the Senate and House of Representatives, open all the certificates and the votes shall then be counted;—The person having the greatest number of votes for President, shall be the President, if such number be a majority of the whole number of electors appointed; and if no person have such majority, then from the persons having the highest numbers not exceeding three on the list of those voted for as President, the House of Representatives shall choose immediately, by ballot, the President. But in choosing the President, the votes shall be taken by States, the representation from each State having one vote; a quorum for this purpose shall consist of a member or members from two-thirds of the States, and a majority of all the States shall be necessary to a choice. And if the House of Representatives shall not choose a President whenever the right of choice shall devolve upon them, before the fourth day of March next following, then the Vice President shall act as President, as in the case of the death or other constitutional disability of the President.—The person having the greatest number of votes as Vice President, shall be the Vice President, if such number be a majority of the whole number of electors appointed, and if no person have a majority, then from the two highest numbers on the list, the Senate shall choose the Vice President; a quorum for the purpose shall consist of two-thirds of the whole number of Senators, and a majority of the whole number shall be necessary to a choice. But no person constitutionally ineligible to the office of President shall be eligible to that of Vice President of the United States.

ARTICLE XIII

SECTION 1. Neither slavery nor involuntary servitude, except as a punishment for crime whereof the party shall have been duly convicted, shall exist within the United States, or any place subject to their jurisdiction.

SECTION 2. Congress shall have power to enforce this article by appropriate legislation.

ARTICLE XIV

SECTION 1. All persons born or naturalized in the United States, and subject to the jurisdiction thereof, are citizens of the United States and of the State wherein they reside. No State shall make or enforce any law which shall abridge the privileges or immunities of citizens of the United States; nor shall any State deprive any person of life, liberty, or property, without due process of law; nor deny to any person within its jurisdiction the equal protection of the laws.

SECTION 2. Representatives shall be apportioned among the several States according to their respective numbers, counting the whole number of persons in each State, excluding Indians not taxed. But when the right to vote at any election for the choice of electors for President and Vice President of the United States, Representatives in Congress, the executive and judicial officers of a State, or the members of the legislature thereof, is denied to any of the male inhabitants of such State, being twenty-one years of age, and citizens of the United States, or in any way abridged, except for participation in rebellion, or other crime, the basis of representation therein shall be reduced in the proportion which the number of such male citizens shall bear to the whole number of male citizens twenty-one years of age in such State.

SECTION 3. No person shall be a Senator or Representative in Congress, or elector of President and Vice President, or hold any office, civil or military, under the United States, or under any State, who, having previously taken an oath, as a member of Congress, or as an officer of the United States, or as member of any State legislature, or as an executive or judicial officer of any State, to support the Constitution of the United Sates, shall have engaged in insurrection or rebellion against the same, or given aid or comfort to the enemies thereof. But Congress may by a vote of two-thirds of each house, remove such disability.

SECTION 4. The validity of the public debt of the United States, authorized by law, including debts incurred for payment of pensions and bounties for services in suppressing insurrection or rebellion, shall not be questioned. But neither the United States nor any State shall assume or pay any debt or obligation incurred in aid of insurrection or rebellion against the United

States, or any claim for the loss or emancipation of any slave; but all such debts, obligations and claims shall be held illegal and void.

SECTION 5. The Congress shall have power to enforce, by appropriate legislation, the provisions of this article.

ARTICLE XV

SECTION 1. The right of citizens of the United States to vote shall not be denied or abridged by the United States or by any State on account of race, color, or previous condition of servitude.

SECTION 2. The Congress shall have power to enforce this article by appropriate legislation.

ARTICLE XVI

The Congress shall have power to lay and collect taxes on incomes, from whatever source derived, without apportionment among the several States, and without regard to any census or enumeration.

ARTICLE XVII

SECTION 1. The Senate of the United States shall be composed of two senators from each State, elected by the people thereof, for six years; and each senator shall have one vote. The electors in each State shall have the qualifications requisite for electors of the most numerous branch of the State legislatures.

SECTION 2. When vacancies happen in the representation of any State in the senate, the executive authority of such State shall issue writs of election to fill such vacancies: Provided, that the legislature of any State may empower the executive thereof to make temporary appointments until the people fill the vacancies by election as the legislature may direct.

SECTION 3. This amendment shall not be so construed as to affect the election or term of any senator chosen before it becomes valid as part of the Constitution.

ARTICLE XVIII

SECTION 1. After one year from the ratification of this article the manufacture, sale, or transportation of intoxicating liquors within, the importation thereof into, or the exportation thereof from the United States and all territory subject to the jurisdiction thereof for beverage purposes is hereby prohibited.

SECTION 2. The Congress and the several States shall have concurrent power to enforce this article by appropriate legislation.

SECTION 3. This article shall be inoperative unless it shall have been ratified as an amendment to the Constitution by the legislatures of the several States, as provided in the Constitution, within seven years from the date of the submission hereof to the States by the Congress.

ARTICLE XIX

The right of citizens of the United States to vote shall not be denied or abridged by the United States or by any State on account of sex.

ARTICLE XX

SECTION 1. The terms of the President and Vice President shall end at noon on the 20th day of January, and the terms of Senators and Representatives at noon on the 3d day of January, of the years in which such terms would have ended if this article had not been ratified; and the terms of their successors shall then begin.

SECTION 2. The Congress shall assemble at least once in every year, and such meeting shall begin at noon on the 3d day of January, unless they shall by law appoint a different day.

SECTION 3. If, at the time fixed for the beginning of the term of the President, the President elect shall have died, the Vice President elect shall become President. If a President shall not have been chosen before the time fixed for the beginning of his term, or if the President elect shall have failed to qualify, then the Vice President elect shall act as President until a President shall have qualified; and the Congress may by law provide for the case wherein neither a President elect nor a Vice President elect shall have qualified, declaring who shall then act as President, or the manner in which one who is to act shall be selected, and such person shall act accordingly until a President or Vice President shall have qualified.

SECTION 4. The Congress may by law provide for the case

of the death of any of the persons from whom the House of Representatives may choose a President whenever the right of choice shall have devolved upon them, and for the case of the death of any of the persons from whom the Senate may choose a Vice President whenever the right of choice shall have devolved upon them.

SECTION 5. Sections 1 and 2 shall take effect on the 15th day of October following the ratification of this article.

SECTION 6. This article shall be inoperative unless it shall have been ratified as an amendment to the Constitution by the legislatures of three-fourths of the several States within seven years from the date of its submission.

ARTICLE XXI

SECTION 1. The eighteenth article of amendment to the Constitution of the United States is hereby repealed.

SECTION 2. The transportation or importation into any State, Territory, or possession of the United States for delivery or use therein of intoxicating liquors, in violation of the laws thereof, is hereby prohibited.

SECTION 3. This article shall be inoperative unless it shall have been ratified as an amendment to the Constitution by conventions in the several States, as provided in the Constitution, within seven years from the date of the submission hereof to the States by the Congress.

ARTICLE XXII

SECTION 1. No person shall be elected to the office of the President more than twice, and no person who has held the office of President, or acted as President, for more than 2 years of a term to which some other person was elected President shall be elected to the office of the President more than once. But this Article shall not apply to any person holding the office of President when this Article was proposed by the Congress, and shall not prevent any person who may be holding the office of President, or acting as President, during the term within which this Article becomes operative from holding the office of President or acting as President during the remainder of such term.

SECTION 2. This Article shall be inoperative unless it shall have been ratified as an amendment to the Constitution by the legislatures of three-fourths of the several States within 7 years from the date of its submission to the States by the Congress.

ARTICLE XXIII

SECTION 1. The District constituting the seat of Government of the United States shall appoint in such manner as the Congress may direct:

A number of electors of President and Vice President equal to the whole number of Senators and Representatives in Congress to which the District would be entitled if it were a State, but in no event more than the least populous State; they shall be in addition to those appointed by the States, but they shall be considered, for the purposes of the election of President and Vice President, to be electors appointed by a State; and they shall meet in the District and perform such duties as provided by the twelfth article of amendment.

SECTION 2. The Congress shall have power to enforce this article by appropriate legislation.

ARTICLE XXIV

SECTION 1. The right of citizens of the United States to vote in any primary or other election for President or Vice President, for electors for President or Vice President, or for Senator or Representative in Congress, shall not be denied or abridged by the United States or any State by reason of failure to pay any poll tax or other tax.

SECTION 2. The Congress shall have power to enforce this article by appropriate legislation.

ARTICLE XXV

SECTION 1. In case of the removal of the President from office or of his death or resignation, the Vice President shall become President.

SECTION 2. Whenever there is a vacancy in the office of the Vice President, the President shall nominate a Vice President who shall take office upon confirmation by a majority vote of both Houses of Congress.

SECTION 3. Whenever the President transmits to the President pro tempore of the Senate and the Speaker of the House of Representatives his written declaration that he is unable to discharge the powers and duties of his office, and until he transmits to them a written declaration to the contrary, such powers and duties shall be discharged by the Vice President as Acting President.

SECTION 4. Whenever the Vice President and a majority of either the principal officers of the executive departments or of such other body as Congress may by law provide, transmit to the President pro tempore of the Senate and the Speaker of the House of Representatives their written declaration that the President is unable to discharge the powers and duties of his office, the Vice President shall immediately assume the powers and duties of the office of Acting President.

Thereafter, when the President transmits to the President pro tempore of the Senate and the Speaker of the House of Representatives his written declaration that no inability exists, he shall resume the powers and duties of his office unless the Vice President and a majority of either the principal officers of the executive department or of such other body as Congress may by law provide, transmit within four days to the President pro tempore of the Senate and Speaker of the House of Representatives their written declaration that the President is unable to discharge the powers and duties of his office. Thereupon Congress shall decide the issue, assembling within forty-eight hours for that purpose if not in session. If the Congress, within twenty-one days after receipt of the latter written declaration, or if Congress is not in session, within twenty-one days after Congress is required to assemble, determined by two-thirds vote of both Houses that the President is unable to discharge the powers and duties of his office, the Vice President shall continue to discharge the same as Acting President; otherwise, the President shall resume the powers and duties of his office.

ARTICLE XXVI

SECTION 1. The right of citizens of the United States, who are eighteen years of age or older, to vote shall not be denied or abridged by the United States or by any state on account of age.

SECTION 2. The Congress shall have power to enforce this article by appropriate legislation.

Samples of Forms You Will
Be Asked To Fill Out

FEDERAL BUREAU OF INVESTIGATION
UNITED STATES DEPARTMENT OF JUSTICE
WASHINGTON, D.C. 20537

APPLICANT

1. LOOP

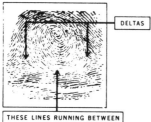

CENTER OF LOOP

DELTA

THE LINES BETWEEN CENTER OF LOOP AND DELTA MUST SHOW

2. WHORL

DELTAS

THESE LINES RUNNING BETWEEN DELTAS MUST BE CLEAR

3. ARCH

ARCHES HAVE NO DELTAS

TO OBTAIN CLASSIFIABLE FINGERPRINTS

1. USE BLACK PRINTER'S INK.
2. DISTRIBUTE INK EVENLY ON INKING SLAB.
3. WASH AND DRY FINGERS THOROUGHLY.
4. ROLL FINGERS FROM NAIL TO NAIL, AND AVOID ALLOWING FINGERS TO SLIP.
5. BE SURE IMPRESSIONS ARE RECORDED IN CORRECT ORDER.
6. IF AN AMPUTATION OR DEFORMITY MAKES IT IMPOSSIBLE TO PRINT A FINGER, MAKE A NOTATION TO THAT EFFECT IN THE INDIVIDUAL FINGER BLOCK.
7. IF SOME PHYSICAL CONDITION MAKES IT IMPOSSIBLE TO OBTAIN PERFECT IMPRESSIONS, SUBMIT THE BEST THAT CAN BE OBTAINED WITH A MEMO STAPLED TO THE CARD EXPLAINING THE CIRCUMSTANCES.
8. EXAMINE THE COMPLETED PRINTS TO SEE IF THEY CAN BE CLASSIFIED, BEARING IN MIND THAT MOST FINGERPRINTS FALL INTO THE PATTERNS SHOWN ON THIS CARD (OTHER PATTERNS OCCUR INFREQUENTLY AND ARE NOT SHOWN HERE).

THIS CARD FOR USE BY:

1. LAW ENFORCEMENT AGENCIES IN FINGERPRINTING APPLICANTS FOR LAW ENFORCEMENT POSITIONS.*
2. OFFICIALS OF STATE AND LOCAL GOVERNMENTS FOR PURPOSES OF EMPLOYMENT, LICENSING, AND PERMITS, AS AUTHORIZED BY STATE STATUTES AND APPROVED BY THE ATTORNEY GENERAL OF THE UNITED STATES. LOCAL AND COUNTY ORDINANCES, UNLESS SPECIFICALLY BASED ON APPLICABLE STATE STATUTES DO NOT SATISFY THIS REQUIREMENT.*
3. U.S. GOVERNMENT AGENCIES AND OTHER ENTITIES REQUIRED BY FEDERAL LAW **
4. OFFICIALS OF FEDERALLY CHARTERED OR INSURED BANKING INSTITUTIONS TO PROMOTE OR MAINTAIN THE SECURITY OF THOSE INSTITUTIONS.

INSTRUCTIONS:

*1. PRINTS MUST FIRST BE CHECKED THROUGH THE APPROPRIATE STATE IDENTIFICATION BUREAU, AND ONLY THOSE FINGERPRINTS FOR WHICH NO DISQUALIFYING RECORD HAS BEEN FOUND LOCALLY SHOULD BE SUBMITTED FOR FBI SEARCH.

2. PRIVACY ACT OF 1974 (P.L. 93-579) REQUIRES THAT FEDERAL, STATE, OR LOCAL AGENCIES INFORM INDIVIDUALS WHOSE SOCIAL SECURITY NUMBER IS REQUESTED WHETHER SUCH DISCLOSURE IS MANDATORY OR VOLUNTARY, BASIS OF AUTHORITY FOR SUCH SOLICITATION, AND USES WHICH WILL BE MADE OF IT.

**3. IDENTITY OF PRIVATE CONTRACTORS SHOULD BE SHOWN IN SPACE "EMPLOYER AND ADDRESS". THE CONTRIBUTOR IS THE NAME OF THE AGENCY SUBMITTING THE FINGERPRINT CARD TO THE FBI.

4. FBI NUMBER, IF KNOWN, SHOULD ALWAYS BE FURNISHED IN THE APPROPRIATE SPACE.

MISCELLANEOUS NO. - RECORD: OTHER ARMED FORCES NO., PASSPORT NO. (PP), ALIEN REGISTRATION NO. (AR), PORT SECURITY CARD NO. (PS), SELECTIVE SERVICE NO. (SS), VETERANS' ADMINISTRATION CLAIM NO. (VA.).

LEAVE THIS SPACE BLANK

FD-258 (REV. 7-13-77)

☆ U.S. GOVERNMENT PRINTING OFFICE : 1980 - 317-188

| APPLICANT | LEAVE BLANK | TYPE OR PRINT ALL INFORMATION IN BLACK | FBI | LEAVE BLANK |

TYPE OR PRINT ALL INFORMATION IN BLACK
LAST NAME **NAM**   FIRST NAME   MIDDLE NAME

SIGNATURE OF PERSON FINGERPRINTED

ALIASES **AKA**

O
R
I

NYINSNYOO
USINS
NEW YORK, NY

RESIDENCE OF PERSON FINGERPRINTED

DATE OF BIRTH **DOB**
Month   Day   Year

CITIZENSHIP **CTZ**

| SEX | RACE | HGT. | WGT. | EYES | HAIR | PLACE OF BIRTH **POB** |

DATE   SIGNATURE OF OFFICIAL TAKING FINGERPRINTS

YOUR NO. **OCA**

LEAVE BLANK

EMPLOYER AND ADDRESS

FBI NO. **FBI**

CLASS _____

ARMED FORCES NO. **MNU**

REF. _____

REASON FINGERPRINTED

SOCIAL SECURITY NO. **SOC**

MISCELLANEOUS NO. **MNU**

| 1. R. THUMB | 2. R. INDEX | 3. R. MIDDLE | 4. R. RING | 5. R. LITTLE |

| 6. L. THUMB | 7. L. INDEX | 8. L. MIDDLE | 9. L. RING | 10. L. LITTLE |

LEFT FOUR FINGERS TAKEN SIMULTANEOUSLY   L. THUMB   R. THUMB   RIGHT FOUR FINGERS TAKEN SIMULTANEOUSLY

U. S. Department of Justice
Immigration and Naturalization Service   **Affidavit of Support**

INSTRUCTIONS

I. EXECUTION OF AFFIDAVIT. A separate affidavit must be submitted for each person. You must sign the affidavit in your full, true and correct name and affirm or make it under oath. If you are **in the United States** the affidavit may be sworn or affirmed before an immigration officer without the payment of fee, or before a notary public or other officer authorized to administer oaths for general purposes, in which case the official seal or certificate of authority to administer oaths must be affixed. If you are **outside the United States** the affidavit must be sworn to or affirmed before a United States consular or immigration officer.

II. SUPPORTING EVIDENCE. The deponent must submit in duplicate evidence of income and resources, as appropriate:

A. Statement from an officer of the bank or other financial institution in which you have deposits giving the following details regarding your account:
1. Date account opened.
2. Total amount deposited for the past year.
3. Present balance.

B. Statement of your employer on business stationery, showing:
1. Date and nature of employment.
2. Salary paid.
3. Whether position is temporary or permanent.

C. If self-employed:
1. Copy of last income tax return filed or,
2. Report of commercial rating concern.

D. List containing serial numbers and denominations of bonds and name of record owner(s).

III. SPONSOR AND ALIEN LIABILITY. Effective October 1, 1980, amendments to section 1614(f) of the Social Security Act and Part A of Title XVI of the Social Security Act establish certain requirements for determining the eligibility of aliens who apply for the first time for Supplemental Security Income (SSI) benefits. Effective October 1, 1981, amendments to section 415 of the Social Security Act establish similar requirements for determining the eligibility of aliens who apply for the first time for Aid to Families with Dependent Children (AFDC) benefits. Effective December 22, 1981, amendments to the Food Stamp Act of 1977 affect the eligibility of alien participation in the Food Stamp Program. These amendments require that the income and resources of any person who, as the sponsor of an alien's entry into the United States, executes an affidavit of support or similar agreement on behalf of the alien, and the income and resources of the sponsor's spouse (*if living with the sponsor*) shall be deemed to be the income and resources of the alien under formulas for determining eligibility for SSI, AFDC, and Food Stamp benefits during the three years following the alien's entry into the United States.

Form I-134 (Rev. 12-1-84) Y

An alien applying for SSI must make available to the Social Security Administration documentation concerning his or her income and resources and those of the sponsor including information which was provided in support of the application for an immigrant visa or adjustment of status. An alien applying for AFDC or Food Stamps must make similar information available to the State public assistance agency. The Secretary of Health and Human Services and the Secretary of Agriculture are authorized to obtain copies of any such documentation submitted to INS or the Department of State and to release such documentation to a State public assistance agency.

Sections 1621(e) and 415(d) of the Social Security Act and subsection 5(i) of the Food Stamp Act also provide that an alien and his or her sponsor shall be jointly and severably liable to repay any SSI, AFDC, or Food Stamp benefits which are incorrectly paid because of misinformation provided by a sponsor or because of a sponsor's failure to provide information. Incorrect payments which are not repaid will be withheld from any subsequent payments for which the alien or sponsor are otherwise eligible under the Social Security Act or Food Stamp Act, except that the sponsor was without fault or where good cause existed.

These provisions do not apply to the SSI, AFDC or Food Stamp eligibility of aliens admitted as refugees, granted political asylum by the Attorney General, or Cuban/Haitian entrants as defined in section 501(e) of P.L. 96-422 and of dependent children of the sponsor or sponsor's spouse. They also do not apply to the SSI or Food Stamp eligibility of an alien who becomes blind or disabled after admission into the United States for permanent residency.

IV. AUTHORITY/USE/PENALTIES. Authority for the collection of the information requested on this form is contained in 8 U.S.C. 1182(a)(15), 1184(a), and 1258. The information will be used principally by the Service, or by any consular officer to whom it may be furnished, to support an alien's application for benefits under the Immigration and Nationality Act and specifically the assertion that he or she has adequate means of financial support and will not become a public charge. Submission of the information is voluntary. It may also, as a matter of routine use, be disclosed to other federal, state, local and foreign law enforcement and regulatory agencies, including the Department of Health and Human Services, the Department of Agriculture, the Department of State, the Department of Defense and any component thereof (if the deponent has served or is serving in the armed forces of the United States), the Central Intelligence Agency, and individuals and organizations during the course of any investigation to elicit further information required to carry out Service functions. Failure to provide the information may result in the denial of the alien's application for a visa, or his or her exclusion from the United States.

U. S. Department of Justice
Immigration and Naturalization Service

Affidavit of Support

(ANSWER ALL ITEMS: FILL IN WITH TYPEWRITER OR PRINT IN BLOCK LETTERS IN INK.)

I, _____, residing at _____
(Name)   (Street and Number)

_____   _____   _____   _____
(City)   (State)   (ZIP Code if in U.S.)   (Country)

BEING DULY SWORN DEPOSE AND SAY:

1. I was born on_____at_____
              (Date)   (City)   (Country)

    If you are **not** a native born United States citizen, answer the following as appropriate:

    a. If a United States citizen through naturalization, give certificate of naturalization number _____

    b. If a United States citizen through parent(s) or marriage, give citizenship certificate number _____

    c. If United States citizenship was derived by some other method, attach a statement of explanation.

    d. If a lawfully admitted permanent resident of the United States, give "A" number _____

2. That I am_____years of age and have resided in the United States since (date) _____

3. That this affidavit is executed in behalf of the following person:

Name			Sex	Age
Citizen of--(Country)	Marital Status		Relationship to Deponent	
Presently resides at--(Street and Number)	(City)	(State)	(Country)	

Name of spouse and children accompanying or following to join person:

Spouse	Sex	Age	Child	Sex	Age
Child	Sex	Age	Child	Sex	Age
Child	Sex	Age	Child	Sex	Age

4. That this affidavit is made by me for the purpose of assuring the United States Government that the person(s) named in item 3 will not become a public charge in the United States.

5. That I am willing and able to receive, maintain and support the person(s) named in item 3. That I am ready and willing to deposit a bond, if necessary, to guarantee that such person(s) will not become a public charge during his or her stay in the United States, or to guarantee that the above named will maintain his or her nonimmigrant status if admitted temporarily and will depart prior to the expiration of his or her authorized stay in the United States.

6. That I understand this affidavit will be binding upon me for a period of three (3) years after entry of the person(s) named in item 3 and that the information and documentation provided by me may be made available to the Secretary of Health and Human Services and the Secretary of Agriculture, who may make it available to a public assistance agency.

7. That I am employed as, or engaged in the business of _____with _____
                                      (Type of Business)   (Name of concern)

at _____   _____   _____   _____
    (Street and Number)   (City)   (State)   (Zip Code)

I derive an annual income of *(if self-employed, I have attached a copy of my last income tax return or report of commercial rating concern which I certify to be true and correct to the best of my knowledge and belief. See instruction for nature of evidence of net worth to be submitted.)* $_____

I have on deposit in savings banks in the United States $_____

I have other personal property, the reasonable value of which is $_____

Form I-134 (Rev. 12-1-84) Y   **OVER**

I have stocks and bonds with the following market value, as indicated on the attached list
which I certify to be true and correct to the best of my knowledge and belief. $ _____
I have life insurance in the sum of $ _____
With a cash surrender value of $ _____
I own real estate valued at $ _____
With mortgages or other encumbrances thereon amounting to $ _____

Which is located at_____
(Street and Number)   (City)   (State)   (Zip Code)

8. That the following persons are dependent upon me for support: *(Place an "X" in the appropriate column to indicate whether the person named is **wholly** or **partially** dependent upon you for support.)*

Name of Person	Wholly Dependent	Partially Dependent	Age	Relationship to Me

9. That I have previously submitted affidavit(s) of support for the following person(s). If none, state *"None"*

Name _____ Date submitted _____
_____
_____

10. That I have submitted visa petition(s) to the Immigration and Naturalization Service on behalf of the following person(s). If none, state none.

Name _____ Relationship _____ Date submitted _____
_____
_____
_____

11. *(Complete this block only if the person named in item 3 will be in the United States temporarily.)*
That I ☐ do intend   ☐ do not   intend, to make specific contributions to the support of the person named in item 3. (*If you check "do intend", indicate the exact nature and duration of the contributions. For example, if you intend to furnish room and board, state for how long and, if money, state the amount in United States dollars and state whether it is to be given in a lump sum, weekly, or monthly, or for how long.)*

_____
_____
_____

OATH OR AFFIRMATION OF DEPONENT

I acknowledge at that I have read Part III of the Instructions, Sponsor and Alien Liability, and am aware of my responsibilities as an immigrant sponsor under the Social Security Act, as amended, and the Food Stamp Act, as amended.

I swear (affirm) that I know the contents of this affidavit signed by me and the statements are true and correct.

Signature of deponent _____

Subscribed and sworn to (affirmed) before me this _____day of _____ .19_____

at _____ .My commission expires on _____

Signature of Officer Administering Oath _____ Title _____

If affidavit prepared by other than deponent, please complete the following: I declare that this document was prepared by me at the request of the deponent and is based on all information of which I have knowledge.

_____
(Signature)   *(Address)*   *(Date)*

U.S. Department of Justice
Immigration and Naturalization Service

Application to Adjust Status from Temporary to Permanent Resident
(Under Section 245 A of Public Law 99-603)

Please read instructions: fee will not be refunded.	Fee Stamp
INS Use: Bar Code	

Address Label

(Place adhesive address label here from booklet **or** fill in name and address, and A 90 million file number in appropriate blocks.)	Applicant's File No. A - 9 _ _ _ _ _ _ _

1. Family Name *(Last Name in CAPITAL Letters) (See instructions)* *(First Name)* *(Middle Name)*	2. Sex ☐ Male ☐ Female

3. Name as it appears on Temporary Resident Card *(I-688)* if different from above.	4. Phone No.'s *(Include Area Codes)* Home: Work:

5. Reason for difference in name *(See instructions)*

6. Home Address *(No. and Street)*	*(Apt. No.)*	*(City)*	*(State)*	*(Zip Code)*

7. Mailing Address *(if different)*	*(Apt. No.)*	*(City)*	*(State)*	*(Zip Code)*

8. Place of Birth *(City or Town)*	*(County, Province or State)* *(Country)*	9. Date of Birth *(Month/Day/Year)*

10. Your Mother's First Name	11. Your Father's First Name	12. Enter your Social Security Number _ _ _ - _ _ - _ _ _ _

13. Absences from the United States since becoming a Temporary Resident Alien. *(List most recent first.)* *(If you have a single absence in excess of 30 days or the total of all your absences exceeds 90 days, explain and attach any relevant information).*

Country	Purpose of Trip	From *(Month/Day/Year)*	To *(Month/Day/Year)*	Total Days Absent

14. When applying for temporary resident alien status, I
☐ did ☐ did not submit a medical examination form (I-693) with my application that included a serologic (blood) test for human immunodeficiency virus (HIV) infection. *(If you did not, submit a medical examination form (I-693) with this application that includes a serologic test for HIV.)*

15. Since becoming a temporary resident alien, I
☐ have ☐ have not been arrested, convicted or confined in a prison. *(If you have, provide the date(s), place(s), specific charge(s) and attach any relevant information.)*

16. Since becoming a temporary resident alien, I
☐ have ☐ have not been the beneficiary of a pardon, amnesty (other than legalization), rehabilitation decree, other act of clemency or similar action. *(If you have, explain and attach any relevant documentation.)*

17. Since becoming a temporary resident alien, I
☐ have ☐ have not received public assistance from any source, including but not limited to, the United States Government, any state, county, city or municipality. *(If you have, explain, including the name(s) and Social Security Number(s) used and attach any relevant information.)*

18. Concerning the requirement of minimal understanding of ordinary English and a knowledge and understanding of the history and government of the United States: (*Check appropriate block under Section A or B.*)

A. I will satisfy these requirements by;
- ☐ Examination at the time of interview for permanent residence.
- ☐ Satisfactorily pursuing a course of study recognized by the Attorney General.

B. I have satisfied these requirements by;
- ☐ Having satisfactorily pursued a course of study recognized by the Attorney General (*please attach appropriate documentation*).
- ☐ Exemption, in that I am 65 years of age or older, under the age of 16, or I am physically unable to comply. (*If physically unable to comply, explain and attach relevant documentation.*)

19. Applicants for status as Permanent Residents must establish that they are not excludable from the United States under the following provisions of section 212 of the INA. An applicant who is excludable under a provision of section 212 (a) which may not be waived is ineligible for permanent resident status. An applicant who is excludable under a provision of section 212 (a) which may be waived may, if otherwise eligible, be granted permanent resident status, if an application for waiver on form I-690 is filed and approved.

A. Grounds for exclusion which *may not be waived:*
- Listed by paragraph number of section 212 (a);

____ (9) Aliens who have committed or who have been convicted of a crime involving moral turpitude (does not include minor traffic violations).

____ (10) Aliens who have been convicted of two or more offenses for which the aggregate sentences to confinement actually imposed were five years or more.

____ (15) Aliens likely to become a public charge.

____ (23) Aliens who have been convicted of a violation of any law or regulation relating to narcotic drugs or marihuana, or who have been illicit traffickers in narcotic drugs or marihuana.

____ (27) Aliens who intend to engage in activities prejudicial to the national interests or unlawful activities of a subversive nature.

____ (28) Aliens who are or at any time have been anarchists, or members of or affiliated with any Communist or other totalitarian party, including any subdivision or affiliate thereof.

____ (29) Aliens who have advocated or taught, either by personal utterance, or by means of any written matter, or through affiliation with an organization:
1) Opposition to organized government;
2) The overthrow of government by force or violence;
3) The assaulting or killing of government officials because of their official character;
4) The unlawful destruction of property;
5) Sabotage, or;
6) The doctrines of world communism, or the establishment of a totalitarian dictatorship in the United States.

____ (33) Aliens who, during the period beginning on March 23, 1933, and ending on May 8, 1945, under the direction of, and in association with:
1) The Nazi government in Germany;
2) Any government in any area occupied by the military forces of the Nazi government in Germany;
3) Any government established with the assistance or cooperation of the Nazi government of Germany;
4) Any government which was an ally of the Nazi government of Germany;
ordered, incited, assisted or otherwise participated in the persecution of any person because of race, religion, national origin, or political opinion.
- Provisions of 212 (e):

____ Aliens who at any time were exchange visitors subject to the two-year foreign residence requirement unless the requirement has been satisfied or waived pursuant to the provisions of section 212 (e) of the Act. (Does not apply to the Extended Voluntary Departure (EVD) class of temporary resident aliens).

Do any of the above classes apply to you?
☐ No ☐ Yes (*If "Yes", attach an explanation, and any relevant documentation. Place mark (X) on line before ground(s) of exclusion.*)

B. Grounds for exclusion which *may be waived:*
- Listed by paragraph number of section 212 (a);

____ (1) Aliens who are mentally retarded.

____ (2) Aliens who are insane.

____ (3) Aliens who have suffered one or more attacks of insanity.

____ (4) Aliens afflicted with psychopathic personality, sexual deviation, or a mental defect.

____ (5) Aliens who are narcotic drug addicts or chronic alcoholics.

____ (6) Aliens who are afflicted with any dangerous contagious disease.

____ (7) Aliens who have a physical defect, disease or disability affecting their ability to earn a living.

____ (8) Aliens who are paupers, professional beggars or vagrants.

____ (11) Aliens who are polygamists or advocate polygamy.

____ (12) Aliens who are prostitutes or former prostitutes, or who have procured or attempted to procure or to import, prostitutes or persons for the purpose of prostitution or for any other immoral purpose, or aliens coming to the United States to engage in any other unlawful commercialized vice, whether or not related to prostitution.

____ (13) Aliens coming to the United States to engage in any immoral sexual act.

____ (16) Aliens who have been excluded from admission and deported and who again seek admission within one year from the date of such deportation.

____ (17) Aliens who have been arrested and deported and who reentered the United States within five years from the date of deportation.

____ (19) Aliens who have procured or have attempted to procure a visa or other documentation by fraud, or by willfully misrepresenting a material fact.

____ (22) Aliens who have applied for exemption or discharge from training or service in the Armed Forces of the United States on the ground of alienage and who have been relieved or discharged from such training or service.

____ (31) Aliens who at any time shall have, knowingly and for gain, encouraged, induced, assisted, abetted, or aided any other alien to enter or to try to enter the United States in violation of law.

Do any of the above classes apply to you?
☐ No ☐ Yes (*If "Yes", attach an explanation, and any relevant documentation and submit Form I-690. Place mark (X) on line before ground(s) of exclusion.*)

20. If your native alphabet is other than Roman letters, write your name in your native alphabet.	21. Language of native alphabet
22. Signature of Applicant - *I CERTIFY*, under penalty of perjury under the laws of the United States of America that the foregoing is true and correct. I hereby consent and authorize the Service to verify the information provided, and to conduct record checks pertinent to this application.	23. Date (*Month/Day/Year*)
24. Signature of person preparing form, if other than applicant. I DECLARE that this document was prepared by me at the request of the applicant and is based on all information of which I have any knowledge.	25. Date (*Month/Day/Year*)
26. Name and Address of person preparing form, **if other than applicant** (*type or print*).	27. Occupation

Application for Waiver of Grounds of Excludability
Under Sections 245A or 210 of the Immigration and Nationality Act

I-690 Instructions

Please carefully read all of the instructions.
The fee will not be refunded.

1. **Filing the Application**

   The application and supporting documentation should be taken or mailed to an American Consulate if the applicant is outside of the United States and is applying for temporary resident status as a Special Agricultural Worker.

   If the applicant is in the United States, a participating Qualified Designated Entity near your place of residence, or

   The Service legalization office having jurisdiction over the applicant's place of residence or employment.

   If an applicant for permanent residence under Section 245A of the Immigration and Nationality Act, the application should be mailed along with the I-698 application form to the Regional Processing Facility having jurisdiction over the applicant's residence.

2. **Fee**

   A fee of thirty-five dollars ($35.00), is required at the time of filing. The fee is not refundable regardless of the action taken on the application.

   A separate cashier's check or money order must be submitted for each application. *All fees must be submitted in the exact amount.* The fee must be in the form of a cashier's check or money order. No cash or personal checks will be accepted. The cashier's check or money order must be made payable to "Immigration and Naturalization Service" unless applicant resides in the Virgin Islands or Guam. (Applicants residing in the Virgin Islands make cashier's check or money order payable to "Commissioner of Finance of the Virgin Islands." Applicants residing in Guam make cashier's check or money order payable to "Treasurer, Guam."

   A fee is not required if this application is filed for an alien who:

   > Is afflicted with tuberculosis;
   > Is mentally retarded; or
   > Has a history of mental illness.

3. **Applicants with Tuberculosis.**

   An applicant with active tuberculosis or suspected tuberculosis must complete Statement A on page two of this form. The applicant and his or her sponsor is also responsible for having:

   Statement B completed by the physician or health facility which has agreed to provide treatment or observation, and

   Statement C, if required, completed by the appropriate local or state health officer.

   This form should then be returned to the applicant for presentation to the consular office, or to the appropriate office of the Immigration and Naturalization Service.

   Submission of the application without the required fully executed statements will result in the return of the application to the applicant without further action.

4. **Applicants with Mental Conditions.**

   An alien who is mentally retarded or who has a history of mental illness shall attach a statement that arrangements have been made for the submission of a medical report, as follows, to the office where this form is filed:

   The medical report shall contain:

   A complete medical history of the alien, including details of any hospitalization or institutional care or treatment for any physical or mental condition;

   Findings as to the current physical condition of the alien, including reports of chest X-rays and a serologic test if the alien is 15 years of age or older, and other pertinent diagnostic tests; and

   Findings as to the current mental condition of the alien, with information as to prognosis and life expectancy and with a report of a psychiatric examination conducted by a psychiatrist who shall, in case of mental retardation, also provide an evaluation of intelligence.

   For an alien with a past history of mental illness, the medical report shall also contain available information on which the United States Public Health Service can base a finding as to whether the alien has been free of such mental illness for a period of time sufficient in the light of such history to demonstrate recovery.

   The medical report will be referred to the United States Public Health Service for review and, if found acceptable, the alien will be required to submit such additional assurances as the United States Public Health Service may deem necessary in his or her particular case.

U.S. Department of Justice
Immigration and Naturalization Service

Application for Waiver of Grounds of Excludability
(Sec. 245A or Sec. 210 of the Immigration and Nationality Act)

Please begin with item #1, after carefully reading the instructions.

The block below is for *Government Use Only.*

Name and Location (City or Town) of Qualified Designated Entity	Fee Stamp
	Fee Receipt No. (This application)

Qualified Designated Entity I.D. No.	File No. (This applicant) A -

Applicant: Do not write above this line. See instructions before filling in application. If you need more space to answer fully any question on this form, use a separate sheet and identify each answer with the number of the corresponding question. *Fill in with typewriter or print in block letters in ink.*

1. **Family Name** *(Last Name in CAPITAL Letters)*   *(First Name)*   *(Middle Name)*

2. **Date of Birth** *(Month/Day/Year)*

3. **Address** *(No. and Street)*   *(Apt. No.)*   *(City/Town)*   *(State/Country)*   *(ZIP/Postal Code)*

4. **Place of Birth** *(City or Town and County, Province or State)*   *(Country)*

5. **Social Security Number**

6. **Date of visa application** *(Month/Day/Year)*—for: ☐ Permanent ☐ Temporary Residence

7. **Visa applied for at:**

8. **I am inadmissable under Section(s):**
   ☐ 212 (a) (1)   ☐ 212 (a) (6)   ☐ 212 (a) (19)
   ☐ 212 (a) (3)   ☐ 212 (a) (12)   ☐ Other 212 (a) *Specify Section* (_____)

9. List reasons of excludability; if active or suspected tuberculosis, the reverse of the page must be completed.

10. List all immediate relatives in the United States (parents, spouse and children):

Name	Address	Relationship	Immigration Status

11. **I should be granted a waiver because:** *(Describe family unity considerations or humanitarian or public interest reasons for granting a waiver).* If more space is needed attach an additional sheet.

12. **Applicant's Signature**

13. **Date** *(Month/Day/Year)*

I&NS USE ONLY
Recommended by:
(Print or Type Name and Title) _____   Date _____

Signature _____   I.D.# _____   Director, Regional Processing Facility _____

Form I-690 (02/14/87)

A. APPLICANT

Instructions: Leave this side *blank* if your Application for Waiver of Grounds of Excludability is for any reason *other than* active or suspected *tuberculosis*. If your application is due to active or suspected tuberculosis, take this form to any physician or medical facility under contract with the Immigration and Naturalization Service. Have the physician complete Section B. You must sign Section A (below) *in the presence of the physician.*

If medical care will be provided by a physician who checked Box 3 or 4 in Section B, have Section C completed by the local or State Health Officer who has jurisdiction in the area where you reside. Present the form to the Health Officer after Sections A and B on this side, and *all sections on the other side* have been completed.

Statement: I have reported to the physician or health facility named in Section B; have presented all X-Rays used in the Legalization medical examination to substantiate diagnosis; will submit to such examinations, treatment, isolation, and medical regimen as may be required; and will remain under the prescribed treatment or observation whether on inpatient or outpatient basis, until discharged at the discretion of the physician named, or a physician representing the facility named in Section B. Satisfactory financial arrangements have been made. **(NOTE: This statement does not relieve you from submitting evidence to establish that you are not likely to become a public charge.)**

A. Signature of Applicant	Date

B. PHYSICIAN OR HEALTH FACILITY

Instructions: This section of Form I-690 may be executed by a physician in private practice (under contract with the Immigration and Naturalization Service), or a physician employed by a health department, other public health facility, or military hospital.

Complete Section B (below) of this form, and have alien sign and date Section A (above) *in your presence. Please be sure the alien's signature above, and the alien's signature on the other side of this form* **are identical.**

Statement: I agree to supply any treatment or observation necessary for the proper management of the alien's tuberculous condition. I agree to submit Form CDC 75.18 to the health officer named below (*Section C) within thirty (30) days of the alien's reporting for care, indicating presumptive diagnosis, test results, and plans for future care of the alien. Satisfactory financial arrangements have been made.

I represent *(enter X in the appropriate box and type or legibly print name and address of facility):*

1. ☐ Local Health Department
2. ☐ Military Hospital
3. ☐ Other Public Health Facility
4. ☐ Private Practice or Private Health Facility under contract with the Immigration and Naturalization Service.

B. Signature of Physician	Date

Print or Type Name and Address of Physician and Facility. (If military, enter name and address of receiving hospital and mail directly to Centers for Disease Control, Atlanta, GA 30333.)

C. LOCAL OR STATE HEALTH OFFICER

Instructions: If the facility or physician who signed in Section B is not in your health jurisdiction and is not familiar to you, you may wish to contact the health officer responsible for the jurisdiction of the facility or physician prior to endorsing this document.

Statement: This endorsement signifies recognition of the physician or facility for the purpose of providing care for tuberculosis.

C. Signature of Health Officer	Date

Print or Type Name of Health Officer*, and Offical Name and Complete Address of Local Health Department.

Form I-690 (02/14/87)

Instructions To Alien Applying for Adjustment of Status

A medical examination is necessary as part of your application for adjustment of status. Please communicate immediately with one of the physicians on the attached list to arrange for your medical examination, which must be completed before your status can be adjusted. The purpose of the medical examination is to determine if you have certain health conditions which may need further follow-up. The information requested is required in order for a proper evaluation to be made of your health status. The results of your examination will be provided to an Immigration officer and may be shared with health departments and other public health or cooperating medical authorities. All expenses in connection with this examination must be paid by you.

The examining physician may refer you to your personal physician or a local public health department and you must comply with some health follow-up or treatment recommendations for certain health conditions before your status will be adjusted.

This form should be presented to the examining physician. You must sign the form in the presence of the examining physician. *The law provides severe penalties for knowingly and willfully falsifying or concealing a material fact or using any false documents in connection with this medical examination. The medical examination must be completed in order for us to process your application.*

Medical Examination and Health Information

A medical examination is necessary as part of your application for adjustment of status. You should go for your medical examination as soon as possible. You will have to choose a doctor from a list you will be given. The list will have the names of doctors or clinics in your area that have been approved by the Immigration and Naturalization Service for this examination. You must pay for the examination. If you become a temporary legal resident and later apply to become a permanent resident, you may need to have another medical examination at that time.

The purpose of the medical examination is to find out if you have certain health conditions which may need further follow-up. The doctor will examine you for certain physical and mental health conditions. You will have to take off your clothes. If you need more tests because of a condition found during your medical examination, the doctor may send you to your own doctor or to the local public health department. For some conditions, before you can become a temporary or permanent resident, you will have to show that you have followed the doctor's advice to get more tests or take treatment.

If you have any records of immunizations (vaccinations), you should bring them to show to the doctor. This is especially important for pre-school and school-age children. The doctor will tell you if any more immunizations are needed, and where you can get them (usually at your local public health department). It is important for your health that you follow the doctor's advice and go to get any immunizations.

One of the conditions you will be tested for is tuberculosis. If you are 15 years of age or older, you will be required to have a chest X-ray examination. *Exception:* If you are pregnant or applying for adjustment of status under the Immigration Reform and Control Act of 1986, you may choose to have either a chest X-ray or a tuberculin skin test. If you choose the skin test you will have to return in 2 - 3 days to have it checked. If you do not have any reaction to the skin test you will not need any more tests for tuberculosis. If you do have any reaction to the skin test, you will also need to have a chest X-ray examination. If the doctor thinks you are infected with tuberculosis, you may have to go to the local health department and more tests may have to be done. The doctor will explain these to you.

If you are 14 years of age or younger, you will not need to have a test for tuberculosis unless a member of your immediate family has chest X-ray findings that may be tuberculosis. If you are in this age group and you do have to be tested for tuberculosis, you may choose either the chest X-ray or the skin test.

You must also have a blood test for syphilis if you are 15 years of age or older.

You will also be tested to see if you have the human immuno-deficiency virus (HIV) infection. This virus is the cause of AIDS. If you have this virus, it may damage your body's ability to fight off other disease. The blood test you will take will tell if you have been exposed to this virus.

Instructions To Physician Performing the Examination

Please medically examine for adjustment of status the individual presenting this form. The medical examination should be performed according to the U.S. Public Health Service "Guidelines for Medical Examination of Aliens in the United States" and Supplements, which have been provided to you separately.

If the applicant is free of medical defects listed in Section 212(a) of the Immigration and Nationality Act, endorse the form in the space provided. While in your presence, the applicant must also sign the form in the space provided. You should retain one copy for your files and return all other copies in a sealed envelope to the applicant for presentation at the immigration interview.

If the applicant has a health condition which requires follow-up as specified in the "Guidelines for Medical Examination of Aliens in the United States" and Supplements, complete the referral information on the pink copy of the medical examination form, and advise the applicant that appropriate follow-up must be obtained before medical clearance can be granted. Retain the blue copy of the form for your files and return all other copies to the applicant in a sealed envelope. The applicant should return to you when the necessary follow-up has been completed for your final verification and signature. *Do not* sign the form until the applicant has met health follow-up requirements. All medical documents, including chest X-ray films if a chest X-ray examination was performed, should be returned to the applicant upon final medical clearance.

Instructions To Physician Providing Health Follow-up

The individual presenting this form has been found to have a medical condition(s) requiring resolution before medical clearance for adjustment of status can be granted. Please evaluate the applicant for the condition(s) identified.

The requirements for clearance are outlined on the reverse of this page. When the individual has completed clearance requirements, please sign the form in the space provided and return the medical examination form to the applicant.

Form I-693 (Rev. 09/01/87) N

Medical Clearance Requirements
for Aliens Seeking Adjustment of Status

Medical Condition	Estimated Time For Clearance	Action Required
*Suspected Mental Conditions	5 - 30 Days	The applicant must provide to a civil surgeon a psychological or psychiatric evaluation from a specialist or medical facility for final classification and clearance.
Tuberculin Skin Test Reaction and Normal Chest X-Ray	Immediate	The applicant should be encouraged to seek further medical evaluation for possible preventive treatment.
Tuberculin Skin Test Reaction and Abnormal Chest X-Ray or Abnormal Chest X-Ray (Inactive/Class B)	10 - 30 Days	The applicant should be referred to a physician or local health department for further evaluation. Medical clearance may not be granted until the applicant returns to the civil surgeon with documentation of medical evaluation for tuberculosis.
Tuberculin Skin Test Reaction and Abnormal Chest X-Ray or Abnormal Chect X-Ray (Active or Suspected Active/Class A)	10 - 300 Days	The applicant should obtain an appointment with physician or local health department. If treatment for active disease is started, it must be completed (usually 9 months) before a medical clearance may be granted. At the completion of treatment, the applicant must present to the civil surgeon documentation of completion. If treatment is not started, the applicant must present to the civil surgeon documentation of medical evaluation for tuberculosis.
Hansen's Disease	30 - 210 Days	Obtain an evaluation from a specialist or Hansen's disease clinic. If the disease is indeterminate or Tuberculoid, the applicant must present to the civil surgeon documentation of medical evaluation. If disease is Lepromotous or Borderline (dimorphous) and treatment is started, the applicant must complete at least 6 months and present documentation to the civil surgeon showing adequate supervision, treatment, and clinical response before a medical clearance is granted.
**Venereal Diseases	1 - 30 Days	Obtain an appointment with a physician or local public health department. An applicant with a reactive serologic test for syphilis must provide to the civil surgeon documentation of evaluation for treatment. If any of the venereal diseases are infectious, the applicant must present to the civil surgeon documentation of completion of treatment.
Immunizations Incomplete	Immediate	Immunizations are not required, but the applicant should be encouraged to go to physician or local health department for appropriate immunizations.
HIV Infection	Immediate	Post-test counseling is not required, but the applicant should be encouraged to seek appropriate post-test counseling.

* Mental retardation; insanity; previous attack of insanity; psychopathic personality, sexual deviation or mental defect; narcotic drug addition; and chronic alcoholism.

** Chancroid; gonorrhea; granuloma inguinale; lymphogranuloma venereum; and syphilis.

Form I-693 (Rev. 09/01/87) N

U.S. Department of Justice
Immigration and Naturalization Service

OMB #1115-0134
Medical Examination of Aliens Seeking Adjustment of Status

(Please type or print clearly) *I certify that on the date shown I examined:*	3. File number (A number)
1. Name (Last in CAPS)	4. Sex ☐ Male ☐ Female
(First)　　　　　　　　(Middle Initial)	5. Date of birth (Month/Day/Year)
2. Address (Street number and name)　　(Apt. number)	6. Country of birth
(City)　　　　(State)　　(ZIP Code)	7. Date of examination (Month/Day/Year)

General Physical Examination: I examined specifically for evidence of the conditions listed below. My examination revealed;

☐ No apparent defect, disease, or disability.

☐ The conditions listed below were found (check all boxes that apply)

Class A Conditions

☐ Chancroid
☐ Chronic alcoholism
☐ Gonorrhea
☐ Granuloma inguinale

☐ Hansen's disease, infectious
☐ HIV infection
☐ Insanity
☐ Lymphogranuloma venereum

☐ Mental defect
☐ Mental retardation
☐ Narcotic drug addiction
☐ Previous occurrence of one
　　or more attacks of insanity

☐ Psychopathic personality
☐ Sexual deviation
☐ Syphilis, infectious
☐ Tuberculosis, active

Class B Conditions

☐ Hansen's disease, not infectious　☐ Tuberculosis, not active

☐ Other physical defect, disease or disability (specify below)

Examination for Tuberculosis - Tuberculin Skin Test	Examination for Tuberculosis - Chest X-Ray Report
☐ Reaction _____ mm　☐ No reaction　☐ Not done	☐ Abnormal　☐ Normal　☐ Not done
Doctor's name (please print)　　Date read	Doctor's name (please print)　　Date read

Serologic Test for Syphilis	Serologic Test for HIV Antibody
☐ Reactive Titer (confirmatory test performed)　☐ Nonreactive	☐ Positive (confirmed by Western blot)　☐ Negative
Test Type	Test Type
Doctor's name (please print)　　Date read	Doctor's name (please print)　　Date read

Immunization Determination (DTP, OPV, MMR, Td-Refer to *PHS Guidelines* for recommendations)

☐ Applicant is current for recommended age-specific immunizations

☐ Applicant is not current for recommended age-specific immunizations and I have encouraged that appropriate immunizations be obtained.

REMARKS:

Civil Surgeon Referral for Follow-up of Medical Condition

☐ The alien named above has applied for adjustment of status. A medical examination conducted by me identified the conditions above which require resolution before medical clearance is granted or for which the alien may seek medical advice. Please provide follow-up services or refer the alien to an appropriate health care provider. The actions necessary for medical clearance are detailed on the reverse of this form.

Follow-up Information:
The alien named above has complied with the recommended health follow-up.

Doctor's name and address (please type or print clearly)　　Doctor's signature　　Date

Applicant Certification:
I certify that I understand the purpose of the medical examination. I authorize the required tests to be completed, and the information on this form refers to me.

Signature　　Date

Civil Surgeon Certification:
My examination showed the applicant to have met the medical examination and health follow-up requirements for adjustment of status.

Doctor's name and address (please type or print clearly)　　Doctor's signature　　Date

The Immigration and Naturalization Service is authorized to collect this information under the provisions of the Immigration and Nationality Act and the Immigration Reform and Control Act of 1986, Public Law 99-603.

Form I-693 (Rev. 09/01/87) N　　　　ORIGINAL: INS A-FILE

U.S. Department of Justice

Immigration and Naturalization Service

FORM G-325A

BIOGRAPHIC INFORMATION

(Family name)	(First name)	(Middle name)	☐ MALE ☐ FEMALE	BIRTHDATE(Mo.-Day-Yr.)	NATIONALITY	FILE NUMBER A

ALL OTHER NAMES USED (Including names by previous marriages)	CITY AND COUNTRY OF BIRTH	SOCIAL SECURITY NO. (If any)

	FAMILY NAME	FIRST NAME	DATE, CITY AND COUNTRY OF BIRTH(If known)	CITY AND COUNTRY OF RESIDENCE.
FATHER				
MOTHER(Maiden name)				

HUSBAND(If none, so state) OR WIFE	FAMILY NAME (For wife, give maiden name)	FIRST NAME	BIRTHDATE	CITY & COUNTRY OF BIRTH	DATE OF MARRIAGE	PLACE OF MARRIAGE

FORMER HUSBANDS OR WIVES(if none, so state)

FAMILY NAME (For wife, give maiden name)	FIRST NAME	BIRTHDATE	DATE & PLACE OF MARRIAGE	DATE AND PLACE OF TERMINATION OF MARRIAGE

APPLICANT'S RESIDENCE LAST FIVE YEARS. LIST PRESENT ADDRESS FIRST.

STREET AND NUMBER	CITY	PROVINCE OR STATE	COUNTRY	FROM MONTH	YEAR	TO MONTH	YEAR
						PRESENT TIME	

APPLICANT'S LAST ADDRESS OUTSIDE THE UNITED STATES OF MORE THAN ONE YEAR

STREET AND NUMBER	CITY	PROVINCE OR STATE	COUNTRY	FROM MONTH	YEAR	TO MONTH	YEAR

APPLICANT'S EMPLOYMENT LAST FIVE YEARS. (IF NONE, SO STATE.) LIST PRESENT EMPLOYMENT FIRST

FULL NAME AND ADDRESS OF EMPLOYER	OCCUPATION(SPECIFY)	FROM MONTH	YEAR	TO MONTH	YEAR
				PRESENT TIME	

Show below last occupation abroad if not shown above. (Include all information requested above.)

THIS FORM IS SUBMITTED IN CONNECTION WITH APPLICATION FOR:	SIGNATURE OF APPLICANT	DATE
☐ NATURALIZATION ☐ STATUS AS PERMANENT RESIDENT ☐ OTHER (SPECIFY):		
Are all copies legible? ☐ Yes	IF YOUR NATIVE ALPHABET IS IN OTHER THAN ROMAN LETTERS, WRITE YOUR NAME IN YOUR NATIVE ALPHABET IN THIS SPACE:	

PENALTIES: SEVERE PENALTIES ARE PROVIDED BY LAW FOR KNOWINGLY AND WILLFULLY FALSIFYING OR CONCEALING A MATERIAL FACT.

APPLICANT: BE SURE TO PUT YOUR NAME AND ALIEN REGISTRATION NUMBER IN THE BOX OUTLINED BY HEAVY BORDER BELOW.

COMPLETE THIS BOX (Family name)	(Given name)	(Middle name)	(Alien registration number)

Instructions

Read the instructions carefully. If you do not follow the instructions, we may have to return your petition, which may delay final action.

1. Who can file?

A citizen or lawful permanent resident of the United States can file this form to establish the relationship of certain alien relatives who may wish to immigrate to the United States. You must file a separate form for each eligible relative.

2. For whom can you file?

A. If you are a citizen, you may file this form for:

1) your husband, wife, or unmarried child under 21 years old
2) your unmarried child over 21, or married child of any age
3) your brother or sister if you are at least 21 years old
4) your parent if you are at least 21 years old.

B. If you are a lawful permanent resident you may file this form for:

1) your husband or wife
2) your unmarried child

NOTE: If your relative qualifies under instruction A(2) or A(3) above, separate petitions are not required for his or her husband or wife or unmarried children under 21 years old. If your relative qualifies under instruction B(2) above, separate petitions are not required for his or her unmarried children under 21 years old. These persons will be able to apply for the same type of immigrant visa as your relative.

3. For whom can you *not* file?

You cannot file for people in these four categories:

A. An adoptive parent or adopted child, if the adoption took place after the child became 16 years old, or if the child has not been in the legal custody of the parent(s) for at least two years after the date of the adoption, or has not lived with the parent(s) for at least two years, either before or after the adoption.
B. A stepparent or stepchild, if the marriage that created this relationship took place after the child became 18 years old.
C. A husband or wife, if you were not both physically present at the marriage ceremony, and the marriage was not consummated.
D. A grandparent, grandchild, nephew, niece, uncle, aunt, cousin, or in-law.

4. What documents do you need?

You must give INS certain documents with this form to show you are eligible to file. You must also give INS certain documents to prove the family relationship between you and your relative.

A. For each document needed, give INS the original and one copy. However, because it is against the law to copy a Certificate of Naturalization, a Certificate of Citizenship or an Alien Registration Receipt Card (Form I-151 or I-551), give INS the original only. **Originals will be returned to you.**

B. If you do not wish to give INS the original document, you may give INS a copy. The copy must be certified by:

1) an INS or U.S. consular officer, or
2) an attorney admitted to practice law in the United States, or
3) an INS accredited representative
(INS still may require originals).

C. Documents in a foreign language must be accompanied by a complete English translation. The translator must certify that the translation is accurate and that he or she is competent to translate.

5. What documents do you need to show you are a United States citizen?

A. If you were born in the United States, give INS your birth certificate.
B. If you were naturalized, give INS your original Certificate of Naturalization.
C. If you were born outside the United States, and you are a U.S. citizen through your parents, give INS:
1) your original Certificate of Citizenship, or
2) your Form FS-240 (Report of Birth Abroad of a United States Citizen).
D. In place of any of the above, you may give INS your valid unexpired U.S. passport that was initially issued for at least 5 years.
E. If you do not have any of the above and were born in the United States, see the instructions under 8. below. "*What if a document is not available?*"

6. What documents do you need to show you are a permanent resident?

You must give INS your alien registration receipt card (Form I-151 or I-551). Do not give INS a photocopy of the card.

7. What documents do you need to prove family relationship?

You have to prove that there is a family relationship between your relative and yourself.

In any case where a marriage certificate is required, if either the husband or wife was married before, you must give INS documents to show that all previous marriages were legally ended. In cases where the names shown on the supporting documents have changed, give INS legal documents to show how the name change occurred (for example, a marriage certificate, adoption decree, court order, etc.).

Find the paragraph in the following list that applies to the relative you are filing for.

If you are filing for your:

A. **husband or wife,** give INS:

1) your marriage certificate
2) a color photo of you and one of your husband or wife, taken within 30 days of the date of this petition.

These photos must have a white background. They must be glossy, un-retouched, and not mounted. The dimension of the facial image should be about 1 inch from chin to top of hair in 3/4 frontal view, showing the right side of the face with the right ear visible. Using pencil or felt pen, lightly print name (and Alien Registration Number, if known) on the back of each photograph.

3) a completed and signed Form G-325A (Biographic Information) for you and one for your husband or wife. Except for name and signature, you do not have to repeat on the G-325A the information given on your I-130 petition.

B. **child** and you are the **mother,** give the child's birth certificate showing your name and the name of your child.

C. **child** and you are the **father or stepparent,** give the child's birth certificate showing both parents' names and your marriage certificate.

D. **brother or sister,** give your birth certificate and the birth certificate of your brother or sister showing both parents' names. If you do not have the same mother, you must also give the marriage certificates of your father to both mothers.

E. **mother,** give your birth certificate showing your name and the name of your mother.

F. **father,** give your birth certificate showing the names of both parents and your parents' marriage certificate.

G. **stepparent,** give your birth certificate showing the names of both natural parents and the marriage certificate of your parent to your stepparent.

H. **adoptive parent or adopted child,** give a certified copy of the adoption decree and a statement showing the dates and places you have lived together.

8. What if a document is not available?

If the documents needed above are not available, you can give INS the following instead. (INS may require a statement from the appropriate civil authority certifying that the needed document is not available.)

A. Church record: A certificate under the seal of the church where the baptism, dedication, or comparable rite occurred within two months after birth, showing the date and place of child's birth, date of the religious ceremony, and the names of the child's parents.

B. School record: A letter from the authorities of the school attended (preferably the first school), showing the date of admission to the school, child's date and place of birth, and the names and places of birth of parents, if shown in the school records.

C. Census record: State or federal census record showing the name, place of birth, and date of birth or the age of the person listed.

D. Affidavits: Written statements sworn to or affirmed by two persons who were living at the time and who have personal knowledge of the event you are trying to prove; for example, the date and place of birth, marriage, or death. The persons making the affidavits need not be citizens of the United States. Each affidavit should contain the following information regarding the person making the affidavit: his or her full name, address, date and place of birth, and his or her relationship to you, if any; full information concerning the event; and complete details concerning how the person acquired knowledge of the event.

9. How should you prepare this form?

A. Type or print legibly in ink.
B. If you need extra space to complete any item, attach a continuation sheet, indicate the item number, and date and sign each sheet.

C. Answer all questions fully and accurately. If any item does not apply, please write "N/A".

10. Where should you file this form?

A. If you live in the United States, send or take the form to the INS office that has jurisdiction over where you live.

B. If you live outside the United States, contact the nearest American Consulate to find out where to send or take the completed form.

11. What is the fee?

You must pay $35.00 to file this form. **The fee will not be refunded, whether the petition is approved or not.** DO NOT MAIL CASH. All checks or money orders, whether U.S. or foreign, must be payable in U.S. currency at a financial institution in the United States. When a check is drawn on the account of a person other than yourself, write your name on the face of the check. If the check is not honored, INS will charge you $5.00.

Pay by check or money order in the exact amount. Make the check or money order payable to "Immigration and Naturalization Service". However,

A. if you live in Guam: Make the check or money order payable to "Treasurer, Guam", or

B. if you live in the U.S. Virgin Islands: Make the check or money order payable to "Commissioner of Finance of the Virgin Islands"

12. When will a visa become available?

When a petition is approved for the husband, wife, parent, or unmarried minor child of a United States citizen, these relatives do not have to wait for a visa number, as they are not subject to the immigrant visa limit. However, for a child to qualify for this category, all processing must be completed and the child must enter the United States before his or her 21st birthday.

For all other alien relatives there are only a limited number of immigrant visas each year. The visas are given out in the order in which INS receives properly filed petitions. To be considered properly filed, a petition must be completed accurately and signed, the required documents must be attached, and the fee must be paid.

For a monthly update on dates for which immigrant visas are available, you may call (202) 633-1514

13. What are the penalties for submitting false information?

Title 18, United States Code, Section 1001 states that whoever willfully and knowingly falsifies a material fact, makes a false statement, or makes use of a false document will be fined up to $10,000 or imprisoned up to five years, or both.

14. What is our authority for collecting this information?

We request the information on this form to carry out the immigration laws contained in Title 8, United States Code, Section 1154(a). We need this information to determine whether a person is eligible for immigration benefits. The information you provide may also be disclosed to other federal, state, local, and foreign law enforcement and regulatory agencies during the course of the investigation required by this Service. You do not have to give this information. However, if you refuse to give some or all of it, your petition may be denied.

It is not possible to cover all the conditions for eligibility or to give instructions for every situation. If you have carefully read all the instructions and still have questions, please contact your nearest INS office.

C. (Continued) Information about your alien relative

16. List husband/wife and all children of your relative (if your relative is your husband/wife, list only his or her children)

Name	Relationship	Date of Birth	Country of Birth

17. Address in the United States where your relative intends to reside

(Number and Street)	(Town or City)	(State)

18. Your relative's address abroad

(Number and Street)	(Town or City)	(Province)	(Country)

19. If your relative's native alphabet is other than Roman letters, write his/her name and address abroad in the native alphabet:

(Name)	(Number and Street)	(Town or City)	(Province)	(Country)

20. If filing for your husband/wife, give last address at which you lived together:

					From		To	
(Number and Street)	(Apt. No.)	(Town or City)	(State or Province)	(Country)	(Month)	(Year)	(Month)	(Year)

21. Check the appropriate box below and give the information required for the box you checked:

☐ Your relative will apply for a visa abroad at the American Consulate in _____
  (City)   (Country)

☐ Your relative is in the United States and will apply for adjustment of status to that of a lawful permanent resident in the office of the Immigration and Naturalization Service at _____ . If your relative is not eligible for adjustment of status, he or she
  (City)   (State)

will apply for a visa abroad at the American Consulate in _____
  (City)   (Country)

D. Other Information

1. If separate petitions are also being submitted for other relatives, give names of each and relationship.

2. Have you ever filed a petition for this or any other alien before? ☐ Yes ☐ No
   If "Yes" give name, place and date of filing, and result.

Warning: The INS investigates claimed relationships and checks whether documents are real. The INS seeks criminal prosecutions when family relationships are falsified to obtain visas.

Penalties: You may, by law, be fined up to $10,000, imprisoned up to five years, or both, for knowingly and willfully falsifying or concealing a material fact or using any false document in submitting this petition.

Your Certification

I certify, under penalty of perjury under the laws of the United States of America, that the foregoing is true and correct. Furthermore, I authorize the release of any information from my records which the Immigration and Naturalization Service needs to determine eligibility for the benefit that I am seeking.

Signature _____ Date _____ Phone Number _____

Signature of Person Preparing Form if Other than Above

I declare that I prepared this document at the request of the person above and that it is based on all information of which I have any knowledge.

(Print Name)	(Address)	(Signature)	(Date)

G-28 ID Number _____

Volag Number _____

I-130

U.S. Department of Justice
Immigration and Naturalization Service (INS)

Petition for Alien Relative

OMB No. 1115-0054

DO NOT WRITE IN THIS BLOCK

Case ID#	Action Stamp	Fee Stamp
A#		
G-28 or Volag#		

Section of Law
- ☐ 201 (b) spouse ☐ 203 (a)(1)
- ☐ 201 (b) child ☐ 203 (a)(2)
- ☐ 201 (b) parent ☐ 203 (a)(4)
- ☐ 203 (a)(5)

AM CON: _____

Petition was filed on _____ (priority date)
- ☐ Personal Interview ☐ Previously Forwarded
- ☐ Document Check ☐ Stateside Criteria
- ☐ Field Investigations ☐ I-485 Simultaneously

REMARKS

A. Relationship

1. The alien relative is my:
☐ Husband/Wife ☐ Parent ☐ Brother/Sister ☐ Child

2. Are you related by adoption?
☐ Yes ☐ No

B. Information about you

1. Name (Family name in CAPS) (First) (Middle)

2. Address (Number and Street) (Apartment Number)

(Town or City) (State/Country) (ZIP/Postal Code)

3. Place of Birth (Town or City) (State/Country)

4. Date of Birth (Mo/Day/Yr)

5. Sex
☐ Male
☐ Female

6. Marital Status
☐ Married ☐ Single
☐ Widowed ☐ Divorced

7. Other Names Used (including maiden name)

8. Date and Place of Present Marriage (if married)

9. Social Security Number

10. Alien Registration Number (if any)

11. Names of Prior Husbands/Wives   12. Date(s) Marriage(s) Ended

13. If you are a U.S. citizen, complete the following:
My citizenship was acquired through (check one)

☐ Birth in the U.S
☐ Naturalization
Give number of certificate, date and place it was issued

☐ Parents
Have you obtained a certificate of citizenship in your own name?
☐ Yes ☐ No
If "Yes", give number of certificate, date and place it was issued

14. If you are a lawful permanent resident alien, complete the following.
Date and place of admission for, or adjustment to, lawful permanent residence

C. Information about your alien relative

1. Name (Family name in CAPS) (First) (Middle)

2. Address (Number and Street) (Apartment Number)

(Town or City) (State/Country) (ZIP/Postal Code)

3. Place of Birth (Town or City) (State/Country)

4. Date of Birth (Mo/Day/Yr)

5. Sex
☐ Male
☐ Female

6. Marital Status
☐ Married ☐ Single
☐ Widowed ☐ Divorced

7. Other Names Used (including maiden name)

8. Date and Place of Present Marriage (if married)

9. Social Security Number

10. Alien Registration Number (if any)

11. Names of Prior Husbands/Wives   12. Date(s) Marriage(s) Ended

13. Has your relative ever been in the U.S.?
☐ Yes ☐ No

14. If your relative is currently in the U.S., complete the following:
He or she last arrived as a (visitor, student, exchange alien, crewman, stowaway, temporary worker, without inspection, etc.)

Arrival/Departure Record (I-94) Number   Date arrived (Month/Day/Year)

Date authorized stay expired, or will expire as shown on Form I-94 or I-95

15. Name and address of present employer (if any)

Date this employment began (month/day/year)

INITIAL RECEIPT	RESUBMITTED	RELOCATED		COMPLETED		
		Rec'd	Sent	Approved	Denied	Returned

Form I-130 (Rev. 06-23-86) Y

I-130

U.S. Department of Justice
Immigration and Naturalization Service (INS)

Application by Lawful Permanent Resident for New Alien Registration Receipt Card

Instructions

Read the instructions carefully. If you do not follow the instructions, we may have to return your application, which may delay final action.

1. Who can file?

You may file this form only if

- you are a lawful permanent resident of the United States *and*
- you need a new card.

2. What documents do you need?

A. If you have your old card, you must give it to INS with this application.

B. Give the INS two color photographs of yourself taken within 30 days of the date of this application. These photos must have a white background. They must be glossy, un-retouched, and not mounted. The dimension of the facial image must be about 1 inch from the chin to the top of hair; your face should be in 3/4 frontal view, showing the right side of the face with the right ear visible.

Using pencil or felt pen, lightly print your name (and Alien Registration Number, if you know it) on the back of each photograph.

3. How should you prepare this form?

A. Type or print legibly in ink.

B. If you need extra space to complete any item, attach a continuation sheet, indicate the item number, and date and sign each sheet.

C. Answer all questions fully and accurately. If any item does not apply, please write "N/A."

4. Where should you file this form?

A. If you are in the United States, take this application form **in person** to the INS office having jurisdiction over your place of residence.

B. If you are outside the United States, take this application form **in person** to the United States consulate or INS office that has jurisdiction over the place where you are now living.

5. What is the fee?

If you check (a) or (b) of item 18 "Reason for New Card," you must pay $15.00 to file this form. **The fee will not be refunded, whether the application is approved or not.** DO NOT MAIL CASH. All checks or money orders, whether U.S. or foreign, must be payable in U.S. currency at a financial institution in the United States. When a check is drawn on the account of a person other than yourself, write your name on the face of the check. If the check is not honored, INS will charge you $5.00.

Pay by check or money order in the exact amount. Make the check or money order payable to "Immigration and Naturalization Service." However,

A. if you live in Guam: Make the check or money order payable to "Treasurer, Guam", or

B. if you live in the U.S. Virgin Islands: Make the check or money order payable to "Commission of Finance of the Virgin Islands".

6. What are the penalties for submitting false information?

Title 18, United States Code, Section 1001 states that whoever willfully and knowingly falsifies a material fact, makes a false statement, or makes use of a false document will be fined up to $10,000 or imprisoned up to five years, or both.

7. What is our authority for collecting this information?

We request the information on this form to carry out the immigration laws contained in Title 8, United States Code 1304(c). We need this information to determine whether a person is eligible for immigration benefits. The information you provide may also be disclosed to other federal, state, local, and foreign law enforcement and regulatory agencies during the course of the investigation required by this Service. You do not have to give this information. However, if you refuse to give some or all of it, your application may be denied.

It is not possible to cover all the conditions for eligibility or to give instructions for every situation. If you have carefully read all the instructions and still have questions, please contact your nearest INS office.

U.S. GOVERNMENT PRINTING OFFICE : 1986 O - 159-542

U.S. Department of Justice
Immigration and Naturalization Service (INS)

Application by Lawful Permanent Resident for New Alien Registration Receipt Card

OMB # 1115-0004

DO NOT WRITE IN THIS BLOCK

Case ID#	Action Stamp	Fee Stamp
A#		
G-28 or Volag#		

F/P to FBI _____ (Date)

I-89 to TCF _____ (Date)

Status Verified ☐ CIS ☐ A File ☐ I-151/I-551 ☐ Other _____ Specify

By _____ Initials on _____ Date Class _____

1. **Name** (Family name in CAPS)   (First)   (Middle)

2. **Address** (Number and Street)   (Apartment Number)

(Town or City)   (State/Country)   (ZIP/Postal Code)

3. **Place of Birth** (Town or City)   (State/Country)

4. **Date of Birth** (Mo/Day/Yr)   5. **Sex**
☐ Male   ☐ Female

6. **Name used when admitted as permanent resident** (if different from 1.)

7. **Social Security Number**   8. **Alien Registration Number** (if any)

9. **Country of Citizenship**

10. **Your Mother's First Name**   11. **Your Father's First Name**

12. The city you lived in when you applied for your immigrant visa or for adjustment to permanent resident status

13. Your destination (city and state) in the U.S. at the time of your original admission.

14. The consulate where your immigrant visa was issued or the INS office where your status was adjusted to permanent resident.

15. Your port of admission to the U.S. if you entered with an immigrant visa.

16. The date you were admitted or adjusted to permanent resident status.

17. List the dates of all your absences from the U.S. lasting one year or longer since you became a permanent resident.

18. **Reason for new card** (If you check a or b, you must pay $15.00 to file this form.)

a. ☐ My alien registration receipt card was lost, stolen, destroyed, or mutilated. Explain how the card was lost, stolen, destroyed, or mutilated. (Attach the remainder of the card, if it exists.)

b. ☐ My name has been changed. (Attach the decree of the court or the marriage certificate and your old card.)

c. ☐ I am required to be registered and fingerprinted after my 14th birthday. (Attach your old card. You MUST use the fingerprint card Form FD-258, which you can get from any U.S. Consular or INS office.)

d. ☐ I am an alien commuter taking up permanent residence in the U.S. (Attach your old card.)

e. ☐ I received an incorrect card. (Attach your old card and explain what is wrong with it.)

f. ☐ I never received my card.

g. ☐ Other (Explain) _____

Penalties: You may, by law, be fined up to $10,000 or imprisoned up to five years, or both, for knowingly and willfully falsifying or concealing a material fact or using any false document in submitting this application.

Your Certification

I certify, under penalty of perjury under the laws of the United States of America, that the above information is true and correct. Furthermore, I authorize the release of any information from my records which the Immigration and Naturalization Service needs to determine if I am eligible for the benefit that I am seeking.

Signature _____   Date _____   Phone Number _____

Signature of Person Preparing Form if Other than Above

I declare that I prepared this document at the request of the person above and that it is based on all information of which I have any knowledge.

(Print Name)   (Address)   (Signature)   (Date)

G-28 ID Number _____

Volag Number _____

FORM I-90 (Rev. 06-23-86) Y

	INITIAL RECEIPT	RESUBMITTED	RELOCATED		COMPLETED		
			Rec'd	Sent	Approved	Denied	Returned

UNITED STATES DEPARTMENT OF JUSTICE
IMMIGRATION AND NATURALIZATION SERVICE

APPLICATION TO FILE PETITION FOR NATURALIZATION

INSTRUCTIONS TO THE APPLICANT

(Tear off this instruction sheet before filling out this form)

You must be at least 18 years old to file a petition for naturalization. Using ink or a typewriter, answer every question in the application form, whether you are male or female. If you need more space for an answer, write "Continued" in your answer, then finish your answer on a sheet of paper this size, giving the number of the question.

YOU WILL BE EXAMINED UNDER OATH ON THE ANSWERS IN THIS APPLICATION WHEN YOU APPEAR FOR YOUR NATURALIZATION EXAMINATION.

If you wish to be called for examination at the same time as a relative who is applying for naturalization is called, attach a separate sheet so stating, and show the name and the Alien Registration Number of that relative.

1. **YOU MUST SEND WITH THIS APPLICATION THE FOLLOWING ITEMS (1), (2), (3) AND (4):**

   (1) Photographs of your Face:

       a. Three identical unglazed copies, size 2 x 2 inches only.

       b. Taken within the last 30 days.

       c. Distance from top of head to point of chin to be 1¼ inches.

       d. On thin paper, with light background, showing front view without hat.

       e. In natural color or black and white, and not machine-made.

       f. Unsigned (but write Alien Registration Number lightly in pencil in center of reverse side).

   (2) **Fingerprint Chart**—Complete the personal data items such as name, aliases, weight, date of birth, etc. Write in your Alien Registration Number in the space marked "Miscellaneous No. MNO" or "Your No. OCA" and take the chart with these instructions to any police station, sheriff's office, or office of the Immigration and Naturalization Service for fingerprinting. You must then sign the chart in the presence of the officer taking the fingerprints and have him/her sign his/her name and title and fill in the date in the spaces provided. DO NOT BEND, FOLD OR CREASE THE FINGERPRINT CHART.

   (3) Biographic Information.—Complete every item in the Biographic Information form furnished you with this application and sign your name on the line provided. If you have ever served in the Armed Forces of the United States, obtain and complete also an extra yellow sheet of the form, bearing the number G-325B.

   (4) U.S. Military Service.—If your application is based on your military service, obtain and complete Form N—426, "Request for Certification of Military or Naval Service."

2. **FEE.**—DO NOT SEND any fee with this application unless you are also applying for a certificate of citizenship for a child (see Instruction 6).

3. **ALIEN REGISTRATION RECEIPT CARD.**—DO NOT SEND your Alien Registration Receipt Card with this application.

4. **EXAMINATION ON GOVERNMENT AND LITERACY.**—Every person applying for naturalization must show that he or she has a knowledge and understanding of the history, principles, and form of government of the United States. THERE IS NO EXEMPTION FROM THIS REQUIREMENT, and you will therefore be examined on these subjects when you appear before the examiner with your witnesses.

   You will also be examined on your ability to read, write and speak English. If on the date of your examination you are more than 50 years of age and have been a lawful permanent resident of the United States for 20 or more years, you will be exempt from the English language requirements of the law. If you are exempt, you may take the examination in any language you wish.

5. **OATH OF ALLEGIANCE.**—You will be required to take the following oath of allegiance to the United States in order to become a citizen:

(30) My occupation is..

List the names, addresses, and occupations (or types of business) of your employers during the last 5 years?   (If none, write "None.")
List present employment FIRST.

FROM-	TO-	EMPLOYER'S NAME	ADDRESS	OCCUPATION OR TYPE OF BUSINESS
(a) ...., 19........	......PRESENT TIME......			
(b) ...., 19........	......................, 19........			
(c) ...., 19........	......................, 19........			
(d) ...., 19........	......................, 19........			

(31) Complete this block if you are or have been married.

I am.. The first name of my husband or wife is (was) ....
      (Single, married, divorced, widowed)

We were married on.. at.. He or she was born at..

.... on.. He or she entered the United States at (place)..

.... on (date).. for permanent residence and now resides ☐ with me

☐ apart from me at ....
       (Show full address if not living with you.)

He or she was naturalized on.. at..; Certificate No..,

or became a citizen by .... His or her alien Registration No. is..

(32) How many times have you been married?............ How many times has your husband or wife been married?............ If either of you has been married more than once, fill in the following information for each previous marriage.

DATE MARRIED	DATE MARRIAGE ENDED	NAME OF PERSON TO WHOM MARRIED	SEX	*(Check One)* PERSON MARRIED WAS CITIZEN ☐ ALIEN ☐	HOW MARRIAGE ENDED
(a)				☐ .... ☐	
(b)				☐ .... ☐	
(c)				☐ .... ☐	
(d)				☐ .... ☐	

(33) I have..............children: (Complete columns (a) to (h) as to each child. If child lives with you, state "with me" in column (h), other-
   (Number)   wise give city and State of child's residence.)

(a) Given Names	(b) Sex	(c) Place Born (Country)	(d) Date Born	(e) Date of Entry	(f) Port of Entry	(g) Alien Registration No.	(h) Now Living at-

(34) READ INSTRUCTION NO. 6 BEFORE ANSWERING QUESTION (36)

I..............................want certificates of citizenship for those of my children who are in the U.S. and are under age 18 years that are named below.
  (Do)   (Do Not)

(Enclose $15 for each child for whom you want certificates, otherwise, send no money with this application.)

....
      (Write names of children under age 18 years and who are in the U.S. for whom you want certificates)

If present spouse is not the parent of the children named above, give parent's name, date and place of naturalization, and number of marriages

....

(15) The law provides that you may not be regarded as qualified for naturalization, if you knowingly committed certain offenses or crimes, even though you may not have been arrested. Have you ever, in or outside the United States:

    (a) knowingly committed any crime for which you have not been arrested? .... ☐ Yes ☐ No

    (b) been arrested, cited, charged, indicted, convicted, fined or imprisoned for breaking or violating any law or ordinance, including traffic regulations? .... ☐ Yes ☐ No

If you answer "Yes" to (a) or (b), give the following information as to each incident.

	WHEN	WHERE	(City)	(State)	(Country)	NATURE OF OFFENSE	OUTCOME OF CASE, IF ANY
(a)							
(b)							
(c)							
(d)							
(e)							

(16) List your present and past membership in or affiliation with every organization, association, fund, foundation, party, club, society or similar group in the United States or in any other country or place, and your foreign military service. (If none, write "None.")

(a)	...., 19.....	to 19.....
(b)	...., 19.....	to 19.....
(c)	...., 19.....	to 19.....
(d)	...., 19.....	to 19.....
(e)	...., 19.....	to 19.....
(f)	...., 19.....	to 19.....
(g)	...., 19.....	to 19.....

(17) (a) Are you now, or have you ever, in the United States or in any other place, been a member of, or in any other way connected or associated with the Communist Party? (If "Yes", attach full explanation) .... ☐ Yes ☐ No

    (b) Have you ever knowingly aided or supported the Communist Party directly, or indirectly through another organization, group or person? (If "Yes", attach full explanation) .... ☐ Yes ☐ No

    (c) Do you now or have you ever advocated, taught, believed in, or knowingly supported or furthered the interests of Communism? (If "Yes", attach full explanation) .... ☐ Yes ☐ No

(18) Have you borne any hereditary title or have you been of any order of nobility in any foreign state? .... ☐ Yes ☐ No

(19) Have you ever been declared legally incompetent or have you ever been confined as a patient in a mental institution? ...... ☐ Yes ☐ No

(20) Are deportation proceedings pending against you, or have you ever been deported or ordered deported, or have you ever applied for suspension of deportation? .... ☐ Yes ☐ No

(21) (a) My last Federal income tax return was filed............................ (year) Do you owe any Federal taxes? .... ☐ Yes ☐ No

    (b) Since becoming a permanent resident of the United States, have you:

    —filed an income tax return as a nonresident? .... ☐ Yes ☐ No

    —failed to file an income tax return because you regarded yourself as a nonresident? .... ☐ Yes ☐ No

    (If you answer "Yes" to (a) or (b) explain fully.)

(22) Have you ever claimed in writing, or in any other way, to be a United States citizen? .... ☐ Yes ☐ No

(23) (a) Have you ever deserted from the military, air, or naval forces of the United States? .... ☐ Yes ☐ No

    (b) If male, have you ever left the United States to avoid being drafted into the Armed Forces of the United States? ...... ☐ Yes ☐ No

(24) The law provides that you may not be regarded as qualified for naturalization if, at any time during the period for which you are required to prove good moral character, you have been a habitual drunkard; committed adultery; advocated or practiced polygamy; have been a prostitute or procured anyone for prostitution; have knowingly and for gain helped any alien to enter the United States illegally; have been an illicit trafficker in narcotic drugs or marijuana; have received your income mostly from illegal gambling, or have given false testimony for the purpose of obtaining any benefits under this Act. Have you ever, anywhere, been such a person or committed any of these acts? (If you answer yes to any of these, attach full explanation.) .... ☐ Yes ☐ No

(25) Do you believe in the Constitution and form of government of the United States? .... ☐ Yes ☐ No

(26) Are you willing to take the full oath of allegiance to the United States? (See Instructions) .... ☐ Yes ☐ No

(27) If the law requires it, are you willing:

    (a) to bear arms on behalf of the United States? (If "No", attach full explanation) .... ☐ Yes ☐ No

    (b) to perform noncombatant services in the Armed Forces of the United States? (If "No", attach full explanation) .... ☐ Yes ☐ No

    (c) to perform work of national importance under civilian direction? (If "No", attach full explanation) .... ☐ Yes ☐ No

(28) (a) If male, did you ever register under United States Selective Service laws or draft laws? .... ☐ Yes ☐ No

    If "Yes" give date.................; Selective Service No....................; Local Board No................; Present classification.................

    (b) Did you ever apply for exemption from military service because of alienage, conscientious objections, or other reasons? ☐ Yes ☐ No

    If "Yes," explain fully...

(29) If serving or ever served in the Armed Forces of the United States, give branch...;

from........................, 19...... to ...., 19......., and from......................, 19...... to ...., 19......;

☐ inducted or ☐ enlisted at...; Service No...............................;

type of discharge..; ....; rank at discharge.................................;
                (Honorable, Dishonorable, etc.)

reason for discharge..
                         (alienage, conscientious objector, other)

☐ Reserve or ☐ National Guard from.. 19...... to.....................................

FEE STAMP

APPLICATION TO FILE PETITION FOR NATURALIZATION

Mail or take to:
IMMIGRATION AND NATURALIZATION SERVICE

(See INSTRUCTIONS. BE SURE YOU UNDERSTAND EACH QUESTION BEFORE YOU ANSWER IT. PLEASE PRINT OR TYPE.)

ALIEN REGISTRATION
(Show the exact spelling of your name as it appears on your alien registration receipt card, and the number of your card. If you did not register, so state.)

Name ....

No. ....

Section of Law .... (Leave Blank)

Date: ....

(1) My full true and correct name is..
(Full true name without abbreviations)

(2) I now live at..
(Number and street.)

....
(City, county, state, zip code)

(3) I was born on.. in..
(Month) (Day) (Year)   (City or town)   (County, province, or state)   (Country)

(4) I request that my name be changed to..

(5) Other names I have used are: ....
(Include maiden name)   Sex: ☐ Male   ☐ Female

(6) Was your father or mother ever a United States citizen?.. ☐ Yes ☐ No
(If "Yes", explain fully)

(7) Can you read and write English?.. ☐ Yes ☐ No

(8) Can you speak English?.. ☐ Yes ☐ No

(9) Can you sign your name in English?.. ☐ Yes ☐ No

(10) My lawful admission for permanent residence was on..under the name of
(Month)   (Day)   (Year)

.... at..
(City)   (State)

(11) Since that date I have resided continuously in the United States and continuously in the State of.. where I now
live since.. During the last five years I have been physically present in the United States for a total of............months.

(12) Do you intend to reside permanently in the United States? ☐ Yes ☐ No If "No," explain:

(13) In what places in the United States have you lived during the last 5 years? List present address FIRST.

FROM -	TO -	STREET ADDRESS	CITY AND STATE
(a) ...., 19......	PRESENT TIME		
(b) ...., 19......	.............., 19......		
(c) ...., 19......	.............., 19......		
(d) ...., 19......	.............., 19......		

(14) (a) Have you been out of the United States since your lawful admission as a permanent resident?.................... ☐ Yes ☐ No
If "Yes" fill in the following information for every absence of *less than 6 months*, no matter how short it was.

DATE DEPARTED	DATE RETURNED	NAME OF SHIP, OR OF AIRLINE, RAILROAD COMPANY, BUS COMPANY, OR OTHER MEANS USED TO RETURN TO THE UNITED STATES	PLACE OR PORT OF ENTRY THROUGH WHICH YOU RETURNED TO THE UNITED STATES

(b) Since your lawful admission, have you been out of the United States for a period of *6 months or longer?*.......... ☐ Yes ☐ No
If "No", state "None"; If "Yes", fill in following information for every absence of more than 6 months.

DATE DEPARTED	DATE RETURNED	NAME OF SHIP OR OF AIRLINE, RAILROAD COMPANY, BUS COMPANY, OR OTHER MEANS USED TO RETURN TO THE UNITED STATES	PLACE OR PORT OF ENTRY THROUGH WHICH YOU RETURNED TO THE UNITED STATES

Form N-400 (Rev. 11-26-79)N

(OVER)

I hereby declare, on oath, that I absolutely and entirely renounce and abjure all allegiance and fidelity to any foreign prince, potentate, state or sovereignty, of whom or which I have heretofore been a subject or citizen; that I will support and defend the Constitution and laws of the United States of America against all enemies, foreign and domestic; that I will bear true faith and allegiance to the same; that I will bear arms on behalf of the United States when required by the law; that I will perform noncombatant service in the armed forces of the United States when required by the law; that I will perform work of national importance under civilian direction when required by the law; and that I take this obligation freely without any mental reservation or purpose of evasion; so help me God.

If you cannot promise to bear arms or perform noncombatant service because of religious training and belief, you may omit those promises when taking the oath.

"Religious training and belief" means a person's belief in a relation to a Supreme Being involving duties superior to those arising from any human relation, but does not include essentially political, sociological, or philosophical views or a merely personal moral code.

6. THIS BLOCK APPLIES ONLY TO APPLICANTS WHO HAVE FOREIGN-BORN CHILDREN WHO ARE UNDER 18 YEARS OF AGE.

Some or all of your *own* foreign-born children (Not Step-Children) who are not yet citizens may possibly become United States citizens automatically when you are naturalized. This will happen:

(1) If the child is a lawful permanent resident of the United States and still under 18 years of age when you are naturalized, and

(2) The child's other parent is already a citizen or becomes a citizen before or at the same time that you become naturalized. If, however, the child's other parent is deceased, or if you are divorced and have custody of the child, then it makes no difference that the child's other parent was or is an alien.

(3) If your child is illegitimate and you are the mother, only (1) above applies.

(4) If the child is adopted, and was adopted before its 16th birthday and is in your custody.

If you wish, you can apply for a Certificate of Citizenship for any of these children, which will show that they are United States citizens. If you do not want such a Certificate, write "DO NOT" in Question (34), page 3; if you do want such a Certificate, write "DO" in Question (34), page 3, and send the following with this application:

(1) Fee. Fifteen dollars ($15) for each child for whom a certificate is desired. DO NOT SEND CASH IN THE MAIL. ALL FEES MUST BE SUBMITTED IN THE EXACT AMOUNT. If you mail your application, attach a money order or check, payable to *Immigration and Naturalization Service, Department of Justice*. (Exceptions: If you reside in the Virgin Islands, remittance must be payable to Commissioner of Finance, Virgin Islands; and if in Guam, to Treasurer, Guam). Personal checks are accepted subject to collectibility. An uncollectible check will render the application and any documents issued pursuant thereto invalid. A charge of $5.00 will be imposed if a check in payment of a fee is not honored by the bank on which it is drawn. The fee will be refunded if for any reason you are not naturalized in time or the child does not qualify for the certificate.

(2) **Personal Description Form.**—A completed Form N—604 for each child.

(3) **Documents.**—The documents applicable to your case listed in the blocks below. If you want any of the original documents returned to you, and if the law does not prohibit the making of copies, a photocopy of the document should be sent with the original document.

Any document in a foreign language must be accompanied by a summary translation in English. A summary translation is a condensation or abstract of the document's text. The translator must certify that he is competent to translate and that the translation is accurate.

(4) **Photographs.**—Follow Instruction No. 1 (1) and send three (3) photographs of each child. Write the child's Alien Registration Number on the back of the photographs, lightly in pencil.

DOCUMENTS REQUIRED WITH THIS APPLICATION

1. Child's birth certificate.
2. Your marriage certificate to child's other parent.
3. If you or the other parent were married before the marriage to each other, death certificate or divorce decree showing the termination of any previous marriage of each parent.
4. If the other parent became a citizen at birth, birth certificate of other parent.
5. If the child's other parent is deceased, or if you are divorced from the child's other parent, the death certificate or the divorce decree.
6. If the child is adopted, adoption decree.

SECONDARY EVIDENCE

If it is not possible to obtain any one of the required documents shown in the block above, consideration may be given to the following documents. In such case you must present a written explanation as to why the document listed in the block above is not being presented, together with a statement from the official custodian of the record showing that the document is not available.

1. *Baptismal certificate.*—A certificate under the seal of the church where the baptism occurred, showing date and place of child's birth, date of baptism, the names of the child's parents, and names of the godparents, if shown.
2. *School record.*—A letter from the school authorities having jurisdiction over the school attended (preferably the first school), showing date of admission to the school, child's date of birth or age at that time, and the names and places of birth of parents, if shown in the school records.
3. If you or the other parent were married before the marriage to each other, death certificate or divorce decree showing the termination of any person(s) listed.
4. *Affidavits.*—Notarized affidavits of two persons who were living at the time, and who have personal knowledge of the event you are trying to prove—for example, the date and place of a birth, marriage, or death. The persons making the affidavits may be relatives and need not be citizens of the United States. Each affidavit should contain the following information regarding the person making the affidavit; His (Her) full name and address; date and place of birth; relationship to you, if any; full information concerning the event; and complete details concerning how he (she) acquired knowledge of the event.

Dear Family Fairness Applicant:

This letter contains instructions for applying for benefits under the INS Family Fairness Program.

If you are the spouse or unmarried child under the age of 18 of an alien who has already been granted temporary or permanent residence under the Immigration Reform and Control Act of 1986, but you were ineligible to apply for the program itself, you may be eligible for the FAMILY FAIRNESS PROGRAM. You must have been living in the United States since prior to November 07, 1986 and your family relationship to the legalized alien must have been established before that date. You must not have been convicted of a felony or three misdemeanors committed in the United States, and you must be otherwise admissible to the United States.

If the above applies to you, you may apply for voluntary departure and employment authorization under FAMILY FAIRNESS. A separate application must be submitted for each person. By applying for voluntary departure you identify yourself as a deportable alien. If voluntary departure is granted, you will be allowed to remain in the United States for increments of 1 year. A grant of voluntary departure does not authorize one to travel outside the United States. Authorization to travel (advance parole) must be requested in writing from a district director at an INS office. If advance parole is obtained, you will no longer be eligible for suspension of deportation. Employment authorization is also granted in increments of 1 year which will allow you to work legally in the United States. If voluntary departure is denied, you may be placed under proceedings as a deportable alien. This program should NOT be associated with the legalization program as there is no confidentiality protection for the information or documents you submit.

The decision on your application will be made from the information and on the documentation you submit. The application will not be returned to you for additional or missing information. Your application must be complete or it will be denied.

To apply, you must submit a package containing the following items:

1. Form I-817, Declaration, Ineligible Family Member of Legalized Alien;

2. Form I-765, Application for Employment Authorization (if you desire employment authorization) along with a $35.00 Filing Fee; (NOTE: While the instructions on Form I-765 allow for the fee to be paid in cash, it is strongly recommended that a money order or bank cashier check made payable to the Immigration and Naturalization Service or "INS" accompany your package.);

3. Three (3) "ADIT" type photos (See instructions on Form I-817);

4. Documents establishing the claimed relationship (See instructions on Form I-817);

5. Clear photocopy of the legalized alien's I-688 Temporary Resident Card or I-551 Alien Registration Card;

6. Completed Form FD-258, Fingerprint Chart;

7. Clear Photocopy of a document establishing your identity (Passport, I-94 or other INS issued document, Cedula, drivers License, etc.), and;

8. Evidence of residence in the United States from November 06, 1986.

YOU SHOULD RETAIN A COPY OF YOUR APPLICATION PACKAGE FOR YOUR RECORDS.

Submit all documents to:

Immigration and Naturalization Service
Family Fairness Program
P.O. Box 6003
London, KY 40742-6003

You must notify INS of any change of address on Form I-697A. This form is available from INS offices.

You will receive a I-689, fee receipt, after you apply and your application has been accepted. It is recommended you keep the receipt with you at all times. You should not make inquiry to the processing facility in Kentucky since your application will be processed by one of four INS facilities.

(March 1, 1990)

U.S. Department of Justice
Immigration and Naturalization Service

OMB# 1115-0166

DECLARATION - Ineligible Family Member of Legalized Alien

I, the Undersigned,

was born on: (Day, Month, Year) _____

and am residing at: (Street, City, State, ZIP) _____

hereby request voluntary departure by reason of my family relationship to an alien legalized through the legalization or special agricultural worker programs created by the Immigration Reform and Control Act of 1986.

(Check one)

☐ I have resided in the United States since

(Date) _____

and my family relationship to the legalized alien was established on

(Date) _____

and I am otherwise admissible to the United States.

☐ I was born after November 6, 1986 and my parent is a legalized alien.

Applicant's Biographic Data
(Please Print)

Name: _____

Nationality: _____ Country of Birth: _____

Sex: ☐ Male ☐ Female

Prior File Number(s): A _____

Father's Full Name: _____ Date of Birth: _____

Mother's Full Name: (Including Maiden Name) _____ Date of Birth: _____

Husband or Wife's Full Name: _____ Date of Birth: _____

Place of Marriage: _____ Date of Marriage: _____

I declare, under penalty of perjury, that the foregoing is true and correct.

Applicant's Signature (Parent to Sign for Child Under Age 18)

X _____
Date

Legalized Alien's Signature

X _____
Date

Legalized Alien's Name (Please Print)
_____

Legalized Alien's A Number
_____

Legalized Alien's Complete Address (Street Name and Number)
_____

(Apt. Number)
_____

C/O
_____

(City, State, ZIP Code)
_____

Warning: *Penalties for submitting false information -*
Title 18, United States Code, Section 1001 states that whoever willfully and knowingly falsifies a material fact, makes a false statement, or makes use of a false document will be fined up to $10,000 or imprisoned up to five years, or both.

Form I-817 (02/14/90)

Please see instructions on reverse.

Instructions for Completion of this Form
Each person requesting consideration under the Family Fairness program must file a separate form. This includes minor children.

You must give INS certain documents with this form to show you are eligible for benefits of the Family Fairness program. You must also give the INS certain documents to prove the family relationship between you and your relative. You must provide the following documents to prove your relationship to a lawful temporary resident:

- **Spouse of legalized alien:**

  Furnish a marriage certificate between you and the legalized spouse. If either you or your spouse was married before, furnish documents to show that all prior marriages were legally ended (divorce decree, death certificate).

- **Unmarried child under 18 years of age, living with the legalized alien:**

  (i) If the legalized alien is the mother - the birth certificate of the child showing the mother's name;

  (ii) If the legalized alien is the father - a marriage certificate of the parents or evidence of legitimation prior to the child's 16th birthday and the birth certificate of the child showing the names of the parents;

  (iii) If the legalized alien is the stepparent - the child's birth certificate showing the names of both natural parents, marriage certificate of the parent to the stepparent, and proof of legal termination (divorce decree, death certificate) of all prior marriages;

  (iv) If the unmarried son or daughter was born out of wedlock and the father is the legalized alien - the parent/child relationship must be established by providing the unmarried son or daughter's birth certificate showing the father's name and evidence that he supported the child;

  (v) If the unmarried son or daughter is the adopted child of a legalized alien - certified copy of the adoption decree showing that the child was adopted while under the age of 16 years, the legal custody decree if custody of the child was obtained before adoption, and a statement showing the dates and places the child and adoptive parent lived together.

A. For each document needed, present to INS one (1) photocopy. Do not send originals unless requested by INS.

B. Original documents must be presented when and if requested by the Service and may be retained for forensic examination at the discretion of the Service.

C. Documents in a foreign language must be accompanied by a complete English translation. The translator must certify that the translation is accurate and that he or she is competent to translate.

In addition to the documents requested above, all applicants must submit the following information:

1. Completed Fingerprint Card, Form FD-258 must be submitted by each applicant 14 years of age or older. Applicants may be fingerprinted by law enforcement offices, outreach centers, charitable and voluntary agencies, or other reputable persons or organizations. The Fingerprint Card (FD-258) on which the prints are submitted, the ink used, and the quality and classifiability of the prints must meet standards prescribed by the Federal Bureau of Investigation. The card must be signed by you in the presence of the person taking your fingerprints, who must then sign his/her name and enter the date in the spaces provided. It is important to furnish all the information called for on the card.

2. Form I-765 application for employment authorization (if employment authorization is being requested);

3. Three (3) ADIT photographs. All photographs submitted must comply with the following specifications;

Included in your package is Form I-697A, change of address card. It is your responsibility to keep the Immigration and Naturalization Service informed of any change of address. One copy of the form is included in your package. You may obtain additional I-697A Forms from any Service office.

Color Photograph Specifications

◄ Sample Photograph

Head Size (Including Hair)
Must fit inside oval. ►

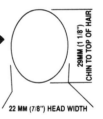

29MM (1 1/8") CHIN TO TOP OF HAIR

22 MM (7/8") HEAD WIDTH

Color films of the integral type, non-peel-apart, are unacceptable. These are easily recognized as the back of the films are black. The acceptable instant color film has a white backing.

- Photograph must show the subject in a 3/4 frontal portrait as shown above.

- Right ear must be exposed in photograph for all applicants, hats must not be worn.

- Photograph outer dimension **must** be larger than 1 1/4^W X 1 3/8^H, but head size, (including hair) **must** fit within the illustrated oval (outer dimension does not include border if one is used).

- Photograph must be color with a white background equal in reflectance to bond typing paper.

- Surface of the photograph **must be glossy**.

- Photograph must not be stained, cracked, or mutilated, and must lie flat.

- Photographic image must be sharp and correctly exposed, photograph must be un-retouched.

- Photograph must not be pasted on card or mounted in any way.

- **Three (3)** photographs of every applicant, regardless of age, must be submitted.

- Photographs must be taken within thirty (30) days of application date.

- Snapshots, group pictures, or full length portraits **will not** be accepted.

- Using crayon or felt pen, to avoid mutilation of the photographs, **lightly** print your name (and Alien Registration Receipt Number, if known) on the back of all photographs.

- **Important Note:** Failure to submit photographs in compliance with these specifications will delay the processing of your application.

Reporting Burden: Public reporting burden for this collection of information is estimated to average 15 minutes per response, including the time for reviewing instructions, searching existing data sources, gathering and maintaining the data needed, and completing and reviewing the collection of information. Send comments regarding this burden estimate or any other aspect of this collection of information, including suggestions for reducing this burden, to: U.S. Department of Justice, Immigration and Naturalization Service (Room 2011), Washington, D.C. 20536; and to the Office of Management and Budget, Paperwork Reduction Project, OMB No. 1115-0166, Washington, D.C. 20503.

Form I-817 (02/14/90)　　　　　　　　　　　　　　　　　　　　　　　　　　　　　　　　　　FPI-PET

Designated Church and Community Groups

Courtesy of the Outreach Program—U.S. Immigration and Naturalization Service.

ALABAMA

Catholic Social Services
211 South Catherine Street, #2
Mobile, AL 36604
(205) 471-1305

ARKANSAS

Catholic Charities
2500 North Tyler Street
Little Rock, AR 72207
(501) 664-0340

ARIZONA

Portable Practical
Educational Preparation, Inc.
1107 G. Avenue
Douglas, AZ 85607
(602) 364-4405

Lutheran Social Ministry
14010 North El Mirage Road
El Mirage, AZ 85335
(602) 937-0500

Central American Refugee Project
1407 North Second Street
Phoenix, AZ 85004
(602) 253-3657

Catholic Social Services of Phoenix
1825 West Northern Avenue
Phoenix, AZ 85021
(602) 997-6105

Catholic Social Services
21 East Speedway
P.O. Box 5746
Tucson, AZ
(602) 623-0344

SER-JOBS for Progress
285 Main Street
P.O. Box 352
Yuma, AZ 85364
(602) 783-4414

CALIFORNIA

World Relief
Primera Iglesia Bautista
2657 Niles
Bakersfield, CA 93306
(805) 324-4020

Metropolitan Immigration
Centers of America
1919 Manolia Boulevard
Burbank, CA 91506
(818) 841-1090

International Assistance
21054 Sherman Way, Suite
265
Canoga Park, CA 91303
(818) 716-0188

International Assistance
4065 East Whittier
Boulevard,
Suite 204
East Los Angeles, CA
90023
(213) 264-7001

Immigrant Legal Resource
Center
1359 Bay Road
East Palo Alto, CA 94303
(415) 853-1600

U.S. Consultation Services
2112 Highway 86, Suites 4
& 5
El Centro, CA 92243
(619) 353-3941

Asistencia Inmigracion del
Condado Norte
935 Mission Avenue
Escondido, CA 92025
(619) 489-8172

World Relief
First Hispanic Church
1304 Mariposa Street
Fresno, CA 93706
(209) 268-4833

International Assistance
Imperial Savings Building
2650 Zoe Avenue, 3rd
Floor
Huntington Park, CA 90255
(215) 585-0764

Los Angeles County Bar
Association
Immigration Legal
Assistance Project
300 North Los Angeles
Street, Room 4349
Los Angeles, CA 90012
(213) 485-1872

Immigration Amnesty
Service, Inc.
132 West First Street, #224
Los Angeles, CA 90012
(213) 613-1250
(213) 613-1295

Catholic Charities
Archdiocese of Los
Angeles
1400 Ninth Street
Los Angeles, CA 90015-
0095
(213) 251-3465
(213) 620-8507

Catholic Charities Center
535 Cooper Road
Oxnard, CA 93030
(805) 487-5567

Alien Legalization for
Agriculture (ALFA)
1601 Exposition
Boulevard, FB-8
Sacramento, CA 95815-
5195
(916) 924-4019

Catholic Social Services
1705 2nd Avenue
Salinas, CA 93905
(408) 422-0602

Catholic Community
  Services
Refugee and Immigration
  Office
4643 Mission Gorge Place
San Diego, CA 92120
(619) 287-9454

Immigration Services of
  Santa Rosa
P.O. Box 4377
606 Chatsworth Drive
San Fernando, CA 91340
(818) 361-4341

World Relief
First Spanish Baptist
  Church
976 South Van Ness
San Francisco, CA 94110
(415) 647-1001

Your Ag Employers Care
1621 East 17th Street,
  Suite S
Santa Ana, CA 92701
(714) 550-0660

Metropolitan Immigration
  Centers of America
6523 Hazeltine Avenue
Van Nuys, CA 91401
(801) 902-9713
(801) 988-8672

COLORADO

Catholic Community
  Services
8715 East Pikes Peak

Colorado Springs, CO
  80909
(303) 636-1537

Justice Information Center
1129 Cherokee Street
Denver, CO 80204
(303) 623-5750

Lutheran Social Service of
  Colorado
Legalization Program
3245 West 31st Avenue
Denver, CO 80211
(303) 458-0222

Catholic Immigration
  Service
Diocese of Pueblo
119 West 6th Street
Pueblo, CO 81003
(303) 543-7837

CONNECTICUT

Catholic Charities
Migration and Refugee
  Services
125 Market Street
Hartford, CT 06103
(203) 548-0059

DISTRICT OF
COLUMBIA

Legalization Assistance
  Center for
  Undocumented Aliens
1118 22nd Street, NW,
  Suite 300
Washington, DC 20037
(202) 223-0283
(202) 223-1811

Travelers Aid Society of
Washington, DC
1015 12th Street, NW
Washington, DC 20005
(202) 347-0101

Congress of Racial
Equality
National Press Building
529 14th Street, NW, Suite
11020
Washington, DC 20036
(202) 737-5030

DELAWARE

Service for Foreign Born
Dover Air Force Base
Personnel Building, Room
120
Dover, DE 19901
(302) 678-6389
(302) 678-7011

FLORIDA

Martin Luther King, Jr.
Farm Workers Fund
1000 C West Main Street
Avon Park, FL 33825
(813) 452-0170

Lutheran Ministries of
Florida
Legalization Services
3565 Davie Boulevard
Fort Lauderdale, FL 33312
(305) 792-6618

Florida Fruit & Vegetable
Association
12175 N.W. 98th Street

P.O. Box 5245
Hialeah, FL 33113
(305) 823-1146

Travelers Aid Society of
Jacksonville
271 West Church Street
Jacksonville, FL 32202
(904) 356-0249

Private Immigration
Agency
7880-B Biscayne
Boulevard
Miami, FL 33138
(305) 751-8212/8217
(305) 854-4950

World Relief
701 S.W. 27th Avenue,
Suite 710
Miami, FL 33135
(305) 541-8320

Catholic Social Services,
Inc.
1771 North Semoran
Boulevard
Orlando, FL 32807
(305) 658-0110

Lutheran Immigration and
Refugee Services
Beth-El Mission
14th Street and Shell Point
Road
P.O. Box 1706
Ruskin, FL 33570
(813) 645-1254

GEORGIA

Latin American
Association, Inc.
2581 Piedmont Road N.E.,
Suite 111

Atlanta, GA 30324
(404) 231-0940

Catholic Diocese of
  Savannah
Office of Social Ministry
St. John's Center
Grimball Point Road
Savannah, Ga 31406
(912) 238-2351

HAWAII

Catholic Immigration
  Center
712 North School Street
Honolulu, HI 96817
(808) 528-5233

Kahili Palama Immigrant
  Service Center
720 North King Street
Honolulu, HI 96817
(808) 845-3918

IDAHO

Ecumenical Ministries
4900 North Five-Mile Road
Boise, ID 83704
(208) 376-4529

Catholic Social Services
St. Therese's Church Hall
125 West 16th Street
P.O. Box 1223
Burley, ID 83318
(208) 678-5453

Idaho Falls Regional
  Information and Referral
  Service
AYUDA Network
545 Shoup Street, Room
  233

P.O. Box 2246
Idaho Falls, ID 83402-2246
(208) 524-2433

ILLINOIS

Catholic Family Center
315 North Root Street
Aurora, IL 60505
(312) 851-1890

The Salvation Army
5040 North Pulaski Road
Chicago, IL 60630
(312) 725-1100

Private Immigration
  Agency
4142 West 26th Street
Chicago, IL 60623
(312) 277-4142

World Relief
3507 West Lawrence, Suite
  206
Chicago, IL 60608
(312) 583-9191

Catholic Archdiocese of
  Chicago
Legalization Outreach
  Services
2380 South Halsted Street
Chicago, IL 60608
(312) 263-4299 (HOTLINE)
(312) 263-4298 (ENG)
(312) 263-4299 (SPAN)
(312) 263-4665 (POLI)

Travelers and Immigrants
  Aid of Chicago
4750 North Sheridan
  Avenue, Suite 200
Chicago, IL 60640
(312) 489-7303

Episcopal Legalization
Center
Chaplaincy Use Book
Store
808 Glenflora Avenue
Waukegan, IL 60085
(312) 244-7676

INDIANA

Catholic Charities
Diocese of Gary
973 West 6th Avenue
Gary, IN 46402
(219) 882-2720

Legal Services
Organization of Indiana
107 North Pennsylvania
Street, Suite 1008
Indianapolis, IN 46204
(317) 631-1395

IOWA

Catholic Diocese of
Davenport
Immigration Counseling
and Resettlement Office
2706 Gaines Street
Davenport, IA 52804
(319) 324-1911

Proteus Employment
Opportunities
1406 Nebraska Street
Sioux City, IA 51105
(712) 258-0094

KANSAS

Harvest America
Corporation
118 Grant Avenue
Garden City KS 67846
(316) 275-1619

Catholic Archdiocese of
Kansas City
Legalization Office (El
Centro, Inc.)
736 Shawnee Avenue
Kansas City, KS 66105
(913) 621-4500

El Centro de Servicios Para
Hispanos
1109 Seward
Topeka, KS 66616
(913) 232-8207

Catholic Social Services
Office of Hispanic Affairs
940 South St. Francis
Wichita, KS 67211
(316) 269-4587

KENTUCKY

Catholic Charities of
Louisville
2911 South Fourth Street
Louisville, KY 40208
(502) 636-9263

LOUISIANA

Catholic Community
Services
1800 South Arcadian
Thruway
P.O. Box 65688
Baton Rouge, LA 70896
(504) 346-0660

Catholic Social Services
Migration and Refugee
Services
1408 Carmel Avenue
Lafayette, LA 70501
(318) 261-5535

Travelers Aid Society of
Greater New Orleans
936 St. Charles Avenue,
Suite 200
New Orleans, LA 70130
(504) 525-8726

MAINE

Catholic Charities
107 Elm Street
Portland, ME 04101
(207) 871-7437

MARYLAND

Catholic Archdiocese of
Baltimore Hispanic
Center
10 South Wolfe Street
Baltimore, MD 21231
(301) 522-2668

Episcopal Social Ministries
105 West Monument Street
Baltimore, MD 21201
(301) 837-0300

Soldier of the Cross of
Christ
Evangelical International
Church
724 Silver Spring Avenue
Silver Spring, MD 20910
(301) 588-8738

MASSACHUSETTS

World Relief
Emmanuel Gospel Center
2 San Juan Street

P.O. Box 18245
Boston, MA 02118
(617) 262-2265

International Institute of
Boston
287 Commonwealth
Avenue
Boston, MA 02115
(617) 536-1081

Catholic Diocese of
Springfield
Refugee Resettlement
Program
11 Pearl Street
Springfield, MA 01103
(413) 732-6365

MICHIGAN

Catholic Archdiocese of
Detroit
Department of Christian
Service
305 Michigan Avenue
Detroit, MI 48226
(313) 237-5900

International Institute
4138 West Vernon Avenue
Detroit, MI 48209
(313) 554-1445

Spanish Speaking
Information Center
2523 Clio Road, Suite 101
Flint, MI 48504
(313) 239-4417

International Institute
11333 Joseph Campau
Hamtramck, MI 48212
(313) 365-1084
(313) 365-1092

Michigan Economic
Human Development
355 East Kalamazoo
Kalamazoo, MI 49007
(616) 343-7126

Catholic Diocese of
Lansing
Migration and Refugee
Services
233 North Walnut Street
Lansing, MI 48933
(517) 484-1010

SER-JOBS for Progress
1535 South Warren Avenue
Saginaw, MI 48605
(517) 753-3412

MINNESOTA

Lutheran Social Services of
Minnesota
Refugee Center
1730 East Superior Street
Duluth, MN 55812
(218) 728-6839

International Institute of
Minnesota
1694 Como Avenue
St. Paul, MN 55108
(612) 647-0191

MISSISSIPPI

Diocese of Biloxi
Catholic Social Services
198 Reynoir Street
Biloxi, MS 39533
(601) 374-8316

MISSOURI

Guadalupe Center, Inc.
2641 Belleview

Kansas City, MO 64108
(816) 561-6885

International Institute of
St. Louis
3800 Park Avenue
St. Louis, MO 63110
(314) 773-9090

MONTANA

Rural Employment
Opportunities, Inc.
1143 First Avenue North,
Suite 217
Billings, MT 59101
(406) 248-8280
(406) 256-1140

NEBRASKA

Nebraska Association of
Farmworkers, Inc.
200 South Silber
P.O. Box 1459
North Platte, NE 69103-
1459
(308) 534-2630

SER-JOBS for Progress,
Inc.
5002 South 33rd Street
Omaha, NE 68107-2594
(402) 734-1321

NEVADA

Catholic Social Services
1501 Las Vegas Boulevard,
North
Las Vegas, NV 89101
(702) 383-8387

Catholic Community
   Services
Migration/Refugee
   Assistance and
   Legalization Services
190 Mill Street, Suite 3
Reno, NV 89501
(702) 323-9005

NEW HAMPSHIRE

Episcopal Legalization
   Center
60 Walnut Avenue
North Hampton, NH 03862
(603) 964-6671

NEW JERSEY

Catholic Social Services
Migration and Refugee
   Services
3098 Pleasant
Camden, NJ 08105
(609) 541-1145
(609) 541-1148

Catholic Community
   Services
One Summer Avenue
Newark, NJ 07104
(201) 482-0100

Haitian Outreach Center
70 Main Street
Orange, NJ 07050
(201) 673-6911

Office of Migration
909 Elizabeth Avenue
Elizabeth, NJ 07201
(201) 352-9700

Office of Migration
380 Monmouth Street

Jersey City, NJ 07302
(201) 653-6515

Hispanic Resource Center
533 35th Street
Union City, NJ 07087
(201) 866-3208

Red Cross of Eastern
   Union County
203 West Jersey Street
Elizabeth, NJ 07202
(201) 353-2500

International Institute of
   New Jersey
880 Bergen Avenue
Jersey City, NJ 07306
(201) 653-3888

National Council for the
   Church and Social
   Action, Inc.
124 North Seventh Street
Newark, NJ 07102
(201) 434-5301

Lutheran Social Services
Roman Catholic
   Immigration Program
189 South Broad Street
P.O. Box 30
Trenton, NJ 08601-0036
(609) 393-3440

North Hudson Community
   Action Agency
507 26th Street
Union City, NJ 07087
(201) 866-2255

NEW MEXICO

Catholic Social Services
Archdiocese of Santa Fe
801 Mountain Road, NE

P.O. Box 25405
Albuquerque, NM 87125
(505) 247-9521

SER-JOBS for Progress
575 Alameda
Las Cruces, NM 88004
(505) 524-1946

Roswell Immigration
  Service Center
213 East Albuquerque
P.O. Box 2663
Roswell, NM 88201
(505) 622-1774

NEW YORK

International Center of the
  Capital Region
West Mall Office Plaza
875 Central Avenue
Albany, NY 12206
(518) 459-8812

Congress of Racial
  Equality
12-06 36th Avenue
Astoria, NY 11106
(718) 361-7437

America's Grateful
  Immigrants
1582 Jerome Avenue
Bronx, NY 10457
(212) 901-0059

World Relief
Joy Fellowship Church
66 East Mt. Eden Avenue
Bronx, NY 10452
(212) 583-9300

Southside Community
  Mission

280 Marcy Avenue
Brooklyn, NY 11211
(718) 387-3803

Catholic Migration
  Services, Inc.
75 Greene Avenue
P.O. Box "C"
Brooklyn, NY 11202
(718) 638-5500

International Institute of
  Buffalo
864 Delaware Avenue
Buffalo, NY 14209
(716) 883-1900

World Relief
First Baptist Church
42-15 Union Street
Flushing, NY 11355
(718) 538-1863

Congress of Racial
  Equality
412 Old Country Road
Garden City, NY 11530
(516) 741-5959

Multi-Cultural Immigration
  Center, Inc.
689 Columbus Avenue,
  Suite 8-C
New York, NY 10025
(718) 492-2459
(212) 663-0753

Movimento de Orientation
  al Emigrante, Inc.
557 West 156th Street
P.O. Box 430, Inwood
  Station
New York, NY 10034
(212) 283-1166
(212) 283-1179

International Immigrants
  Foundation
130 West 42nd Street, 17th
  Floor
New York, NY 10036
(212) 221-7255

Catholic Archdiocese of
  New York
Office For Legalization
  Services
185 Avenue D
New York, NY 10009
(212) 460-8377

International Ladies
  Garment Workers Union
Immigration Project
275 Seventh Avenue
New York, NY 10001
(212) 627-0600

Rural Opportunities, Inc.
346 Broadway
Newburgh, NY 12550
(914) 562-7350

Catholic Charities
716 Caroline Street
P.O. Box 296
Ogdensburgh, NY 13669
(315) 393-2660

Catholic Family Center
50 Chestnut Street, 5th
  Floor
Rochester, NY 14604
(716) 546-7220

Americanization League of
  Syracuse and Onondaga
  County
725 Harrison Street, Room
  209

Syracuse, NY 13210
(315) 425-4120

Westchester Hispanic
  Coalition, Inc.
200 Mamaroneck Avenue
White Plains, NY 10601
(914) 948-8466

NORTH CAROLINA

Catholic Social Services
1524 East Morehead Street
Charlotte, NC 28207
(704) 331-1720

Episcopal Migrant Ministry
P.O. Box 1514
Route 6 State Road 1636
Dunn, NC 28334
(919) 567-6917

OHIO

Ohio Farmworker
  Opportunities
Division of Rural
  Opportunities, Inc.
1616 East Wooster, Suite 9
P.O. Box 186
Bowling Green, OH 43402
(419) 354-3548

Travelers Aid/International
  Institute
632 Vine Street, Suite 505
Cincinnati, OH 45202
(513) 721-7660

Nationalities Services
  Center
1715 Euclid Avenue

Cleveland, OH 44115
(216) 781-4560

International Institute
2040 Scottwood Avenue
Toledo, OH 43620
(419) 241-9178

OKLAHOMA

Associated Catholic
  Charities
Immigration Services
425 N.W. 7th Street
P.O. Box 1516
Oklahoma City, OK 73101
(405) 232-9801

Catholic Diocese of Tulsa
Migration and Refugee
  Services
739 North Denver
Tulsa, OK 74106
(918) 585-8167

OREGON

OHDC-Migrant
Sunnyside Mall, Highway
  395
Hermiston, OR 97838
(503) 567-5800

Immigrants Project
All Saint's Church
372 N.E. Lincoln Street
Hillsboro, OR 97124
(503) 648-4518

Treasure Valley
  Immigration
Counseling Service
772 North Oregon

Ontario, OR 97914
(503) 889-3121

San Salvador Vicarriate
Immigration Counseling
  Service
621 S.W. Morrison, Suite
  205
Portland, OR 97205
(503) 221-1689

PENNSYLVANIA

Pennsylvania Farmworker
  Opportunities Division
  of Rural Opportunities,
  Inc.
310 Lortz Avenue
Chambersburg, PA 17201
(717) 264-2839

International Institute
330 Holland Street
P.O. Box 496
Erie, PA 16512
(814) 452-3935

Nationalities Service
  Center
10 South Prince Street
Lancaster, PA 17603
(717) 291-4454

Philadelphia Refugee
  Service Center
4047-49 Sansom Street
Philadelphia, PA 19104
(215) 386-1298

Catholic Social Service
  Agency
138 North Ninth Street
Reading, PA 19601
(215) 374-4891

PUERTO RICO

Movimiento de Orientacion
al Emigrante, Inc.
Ave Ponce de Leon 1612
Portada 23, Idif Avianca
7th Piso
Santurce, PR 00907
(809) 724-5240

RHODE ISLAND

International Institute of
Rhode Island, Inc.
421 Elmwood Avenue
Providence, RI 02907
(401) 461-5940

SOUTH CAROLINA

Telamon Corporation
1804 C Savannah Highway
Charleston, SC 29407
(803) 766-1545

SOUTH DAKOTA

Lutheran Social Services
601 West 11th Street
Sioux Falls, SD 57104
(605) 336-9136

TENNESSEE

Templo Bautista
1000 South Cooper Street
Memphis, TN 38104
(901) 274-1366

Catholic Charities
Refugee Resettlement
30 White Bridge Road

Nashville, TN 37205
(615) 352-3052

TEXAS

Austin Travis County
Refugee Services
1607 West Sixth Street
Austin, TX 78703
(512) 478-5535

Cristo Vive for Immigrants
7524 North Lamar, Suite
106-10
Austin, TX 78752
(512) 453-8483

Catholic Diocese of Austin
Immigration Legalization
Service
500 Buchanan, Suite B
P.O. Box 763
Burnet, TX 78611
(512) 756-7760

Northcutt Immigration
Assistance Center
Mary King Memorial UMC
2602 Kings Road
Dallas, TX 75219
(214) 528-5827

Catholic Counseling
Services
Migration and Refugee
Services
3845 Oak Lawn Avenue
Dallas, TX 75219
(214) 528-8120

Catholic Diocese of El Paso
Migration and Refugee
Services
1200 North Mesa

El Paso, TX 79902
(915) 532-3975

World Relief
4567 James Avenue, Suite
  B
Fort Worth, TX 76115
(817) 924-0748

Refugee Service Alliance
2808 Caroline Street
Houston, TX 77004
(713) 655-1720

Immigration Counseling
  Center
945 Lathrop
Houston, TX 77020
(713) 924-6045

San Antonio Literacy
  Council
1101 West Woodlawn
San Antonio, TX 78211
(512) 732-9711

Catholic Services for
  Immigrants
2903 West Salinas
San Antonio, TX 78207
(512) 432-6091

Immigration Services
  Consultant
602 East Sixth Street,
  Suite 1
Weslaco, TX 78596
(512) 968-8484

UTAH

Weber Council of Spanish
  Speaking Organizations
369 Healy Street
Ogden, UT 84401
(801) 621-1991

Catholic Community
  Services
Utah Immigration Project-
  Outreach Program
840 Sunset Drive
Richfield, UT 84701
(801) 896-3567

Catholic Community
  Services of Utah
333 East South Temple,
  #701
Salt Lake City, UT 84111
(801) 328-9100

VERMONT

Vermont Refugee
  Resettlement Program
59–63 Pearl Street
Burlington, VT 05401
(802) 658-1120

VIRGINIA

Spanish Speaking
  Committee of Virginia
2049 North 15th Street,
  Suite 209
Arlington, VA 22201
(703) 558-2128

Telamon Corporation
3608 Campbell Avenue
Lynchburg, VA 24501
(804) 846-4100

Frederick Episcopal Parish
  Legalization Center
134 West Boscawen Street
Winchester, VA 22601
(703) 662-5843

WASHINGTON

Centro Campesino
  Immigrant Project
P.O. Box 800
120 Sunnyside Avenue
Granger, WA 98932
(509) 854-2222

Washington State Migrant
  Council
Mabton MHS
North First & B Streets
P.O. Box 128
Mabton, WA 98935
(509) 894-4322

Washington State Migrant
  Council
Moses Lake MHS
Fifth and Chestnut Streets
Moses Lake, WA 98837
(509) 765-6724

Washington State Migrant
  Council
Mt. Vernon MHS
2010 North LaVenture
Mt. Vernon, WA 98273
(206) 428-3993

Washington Association of
  Churches
3902 South Ferdinand
Seattle, WA 98118
(206) 721-5288

Hispanic Immigration
  Program
Catholic Archdiocese of
  Seattle
3600 South Graham
Seattle, WA 98118
(206) 721-4752

Catholic Family Services
West 1104 Heroy
Spokane, WA 99205
(509) 456-7153

Enterprise for Progress in
  the Community
1910 Englewood Avenue
Yakima, WA 98902
(509) 248-3950

WEST VIRGINIA

Catholic Diocese of
  Wheeling–Charleston
Migration and Refugee
  Services
901 Quarrier Street, Room
  201
Charleston, WV 25301
(304) 343-1036

WISCONSIN

Spanish Centers of Racine
Kenosha and Walroth, Inc.
1212 57th Street
Kenosha, WI
(414) 552-7830

The Council for the Spanish
  Speaking
614 West National Avenue
Milwaukee, WI 53204
(414) 384-3700

La Casa de Esperanza
410 Arcadian Avenue
Waukesha, WI 53186
(414) 547-0887

WYOMING

Metropolitan Analysis and
   Retrieval Systems, Inc.
Warland Municipal Airport
Terminal Building Airport
   Road
Warland, WY 82401
(307) 347-2483